# Custer and Crazy Horse

# Custer and Crazy Horse

## A Story of Two Warriors

## Jim Razzi

SCHOLASTIC INC.
New York Toronto London Auckland Sydney

## PHOTO CREDITS

The Bettmann Archive, Inc.: pages 6, 73, 82, 107, 127, 133, 162–163

Custer Battlefield Historical and Museum Association: pages 32, 99

The Granger Collection: page 49

Courtesy of Museum of the American Indian, Heye Foundation: page 76

National Archives: pages 92, 120

National Park Service, Fort Laramie National Historical Site Photo: page 24

South Dakota State Historical Society: pages 37, 53

Wide World Photos: page 64

ISBN 0-590-41836-X

12 11 10 9 8 7 6 5 4 3 2 1          9/8 0 1 2 3 4/9

Printed in the U.S.A.                                    28

First Scholastic printing, April 1989

# Contents

# Contents

# *Prologue*
# *Death at the Little Bighorn*

Colonel Custer and the Seventh Cavalry of the U.S. Army were on the run.

What had started out as an attack on the Indian village situated along the banks of the Little Bighorn River had turned into a frenzied retreat. Worse, the men had dismounted and were fighting on foot.

And now, with their backs against the high ground — their horses dead or scattered by the Indians — the troopers of Custer's undefeated Seventh Cavalry were making a last stand.

They were hot and tired and covered with dust. The air was filled with the popping sound of gunfire, the humming zing of arrows, the high-pitched neighing of excited horses, and the war cries of thousands of warriors as Custer and his men desperately sought to defend themselves.

But the warriors of Chief Gall were pressing them hard. More than two thousand braves had swarmed out of the village like angry bees from a hive when Custer had attempted to attack. He and the five companies with him had been overwhelmed.

The troopers were now strung out on a ridge in the shape of a loose "V" with Custer at its base. Some of the troopers tried to form defensive clusters, but the situation was hopeless. The screaming warriors charging into their midst were cutting them down like shafts of wheat.

But Custer and Captain Yates, one of his officers, were almost at the top of the ridge. If they, and what was left of the Seventh, could reach it, they might still have a fighting chance. . . .

Suddenly, as if out of thin air, a thousand more warriors appeared on the crest of the ridge behind them.

Their bodies painted for war, their faces grim, they seemed the embodiment of death to the trapped troopers below. Even their ponies looked fierce. Painted with red and blue zigzag lightning bolts and other designs, the horses tossed their proud, large heads and seemed to look at the troopers with the same unmerciful gaze as their masters.

And at the head of this painted and terrible horde, one warrior stood out by his relative plainness. He was unpainted except for a red lightning streak down one side of his face, and yellow dots on his almost naked body. A single feather and a small, dried red-backed hawk adorned his long, light-brown hair. Cradled in his arms was a Winchester rifle.

The warrior was the famous Oglala Sioux war chief, Crazy Horse.

Crazy Horse knew the soldiers were finished. He and his men had but to ride down the hill and these troopers of the famed Seventh Cavalry would be no more. If he had any pity in his heart, he brushed it aside. This was the same Seventh Cavalry that had destroyed a peaceful Indian village at the banks of the Washita River eight years ago, killing men, women, and children alike while their band played their regimental tune.

Crazy Horse turned to his braves and raised his arm. "It's a good day to die!" he yelled. A thousand war-whoops filled the air as the warriors whipped their ponies and plunged down the hill. . . .

# 1
# *The Light-Haired Boy*

**T**he paths that had led Custer and Crazy Horse to the confrontation by the banks of the Little Bighorn River were different, yet strangely parallel.

For Crazy Horse, the path began in a peaceful Oglala Sioux village that was situated near the Black Hills on the northern plains of America. . . .

The Sioux were a large tribe with many different branches, including the Oglalas and the Brulés.

In one particular camp, in the year 1842 or thereabouts, a Brulé woman, the wife of an Oglala holy man, gave birth to a male child, who would grow up to be named Crazy Horse, after his father. He was not known as Crazy Horse from birth, however. Indians did not get a real name until they had performed some brave or daring deed or until something remarkable happened to them. Until that time, children were called by nicknames — usually because of some physical trait or habit. Since the young boy had wavy brown hair, he was called Curly.

Curly had an older sister and a younger brother. His family was well respected in the tribe. His father was not a warrior, but a healer. He was also a dreamer and an interpreter of dreams. The Sioux put great faith in dreams and their meanings. Since a dream's meaning was sometimes hard to figure out, it was important to have someone in the tribe who could do that for you.

It seemed right, therefore, that a holy man like Crazy Horse should have a son who, from the very beginning, was different from the other Indians. Instead of straight black hair and dark skin, he had light wavy hair and a light complexion. This was seen as a sign that the boy would become someone special. To the Indians, strangeness meant great potential.

Curly's uniqueness foretold that he might become a medicine man or a chief. But Sioux society never pushed anyone into becoming what the tribe wanted him to be. Instead, the young person was encouraged to find his own way.

Young Curly didn't think about the future just yet, though. He was only six years old and was more interested in tagging along with his older sister and playing games with the other children in the village. Curly was left pretty much on his own — all Indian children enjoyed the freedom to roam around the village and its outskirts at will. The older ones always looked out for the younger ones.

Family games, like making tepees and playing house, were favorites with boys and girls alike. But as Curly grew older, the games became rougher and were played by boys only. These were games that required skill, endurance, and strength — qualities that were needed for survival on the Great Plains.

Shooting arrows from a bow was a major pastime for Curly and his friends. It was said that a

A Brulé Indian camp, late nineteenth century. Curly's camp probably looked very similar to this one.

Plains Indian could shoot five to ten arrows in the air so fast that the last one would be flying before the first one hit the ground.

But the quality that was stressed above all was bravery. It was the most esteemed virtue in every Indian nation. A brave warrior commanded everyone's respect and admiration. Bravery brought some of the highest honors any Indian could hope for.

Curly was well on his way to capturing those honors. Even at the age of ten, he showed great skill in hunting and great courage in the face of danger.

All the young boys in the tribe competed to see who was the strongest, the fastest, the bravest. The words of the men rang in their ears always: "It is better to die young in full health and power then to live a long life and grow old, weak, and helpless." So they growled like grizzlies and whooped and yelled to frighten their enemies and make themselves bold.

As soon as Curly was old enough to take care of it, his father gave him a horse of his own. From then on, there was no stopping him. Now Curly viewed the world as an Indian of the plains, mounted on a swift, sure pony.

Indians loved their colorful brown-and-white-spotted steeds. So much so, that whenever a dull gray or brown horse would fall into the hands of a Plains Indian, the first thing he would do was paint it! But Curly's horse was a true Indian pony and had no need of paint to add to its beauty.

Every chance Curly got, he rode out on the plains, urging his pony on faster and faster. "Yip! yip! *Hoppo!*" He yelled out the cry for charging the enemy as the wind snatched the words from his mouth and tossed them behind him. He loved to feel the strong, wiry body of the pony beneath him as he rode free and wild on the prairie, his long, fair hair streaming behind him like a tattered brown banner.

Curly learned everything there was to learn about horses. He could also do tricks that any circus rider of his day would have been proud of. For example, Curly could gallop past a friend on the ground and pluck him up onto the back of his horse. He also learned how to lie flat on the side of his mount, with his leg hooked over the pony's back so that no enemy could get a shot at him from the other side. Curly even learned how to *sleep* while riding! This was a good thing to know if one had to travel all night without stopping.

And under the guidance of his father, Curly also learned things about the prairie he roamed on so freely. Each morning when he left the tepee, his father would say, "Look around you, there is much to see if your eyes are sharp."

Curly did look and learn. Each evening when he returned, his father would ask him questions. Did he see any animals that day? What were they doing? After Curly would tell him what he had seen, his father would explain the meaning of it to him.

For instance, if Curly had seen a herd of wild ponies walking steadily along, strung out in a line, that meant they were going toward water. If they were loosely scattered about and grazing, they were coming from water. The location of water was one of the most basic things an Indian had to know, no matter where he was in the wilderness.

Curly had great respect and admiration for his father, and he would listen in wide-eyed attention to the holy man's words. Curly was also a good pupil, and it wasn't long before he was sure of his knowledge and his skills. Curly was also sure of what he wanted to be when he grew up. Although he was his father's son in some ways, especially when it came to being a thinker, Curly had no desire to follow in his father's footsteps and become a holy man. Instead, his greatest wish was to become a warrior.

One of Curly's biggest thrills was to gather with the rest of the village as a war party returned from a foray. As the warriors entered the village, they would ride around it a number of times, proudly displaying the fresh scalps and other trophies of war they had taken. As each warrior passed, the old women would scream out his name in honor of his bravery.

Curly watched in wide-eyed wonder. He imagined himself as one of the returning warriors and the old women screaming out his name, "Curly! Curly!"

But he knew that he must be directed by his vision to show him what the future would bring.

It was a Sioux custom for each young male to go on a Vision Quest. This was done by first fasting and undergoing purification rites. After being instructed by a holy man, the vision seeker would then go to a sacred place and remain there until he had his vision.

If the seeker *did* have a vision — which was not always the case — it would tell him what path he should follow for the rest of his life. The Sioux never questioned the vision or dream because they believed it came straight from *wakan tanka* — the Great Spirit.

But Curly was also worried. He knew that wherever his vision led him, he should follow. What if his vision told him *not* to be a warrior? Even worse, what if he dreamed of thunder or the thunder beings? That would mean he should become a *heyoka* — a backwards man. He would have to spend his life doing everything backwards! In the summer he must make believe he was freezing, and in the winter he must complain of the heat. He must ride his horse *backwards*, with his face turned to the tail and his back to the front. He would even have to wear his clothes and moccasins backwards! Although a *heyoka* was still respected in the tribe, Curly did not wish to become one.

"The only way a *heyoka* may become normal," his father would tell him, "is to put his bare arms in a pot of boiling dog meat and pull out the head."

No, thought Curly, he did not want to dream of the thunder beings. But it was worst of all not to even *get* a vision. He knew that not everybody did. And the unfortunates who *didn't* get a vision could never achieve the honor and status of the ones who did.

A vision gave a Sioux a purpose in life; a guiding force for him to live by. Without a vision you were nothing. And above all, the light-skinned boy wanted to be somebody. He wanted to be admired by his people. It was a driving force in him that he could not deny. He *must* have his vision. He must be a warrior!

## 2
# "Autie" Custer

**I**f Crazy Horse and Custer were racing to meet their destinies, then Custer had a head start. He was born two years or so before Crazy Horse on December 5th, 1839, in the small town of New Rumley, Ohio.

George Armstrong Custer was the third child born to Emmanuel Custer, a blacksmith and farmer, and his second wife, Maria. The first two had died in infancy, so the little boy was especially cherished. Maria had been a widow when Emmanuel married her, and each of them had brought children from their first marriages into the union. So little George already had plenty of brothers and sisters to play with.

In contrast to the wild, sometimes bleak, prairie where Curly was spending his boyhood, Ohio was fertile and cultivated. It was called the "Garden of the World" by its residents, and it certainly deserved the name. Forests of oak, beech, poplar, maple, and walnut dotted the land, and the Ohio River flowed clear and sparkling along the state's southern rim on its way to the Mississippi.

Many of the citizens of Ohio came from other parts of the United States, and there was a good number of European immigrants. There was also a large number of freed black slaves who had won their freedom by crossing the river into Ohio from the slave states of the south. It was truly a small American melting pot, and many people found it a natural paradise.

Civilized society, however, took a different view of nature than the so-called "uncivilized" Indians. The Indians accepted the land as they found it and tried to live in harmony with it. Americans, on the other hand, were determined to put it to work. Where the Indian saw a mountain to admire, the American saw minerals to be mined. Where the Indian saw a prairie to run free on, the American saw railroads to be built across it. Where the Indian saw a forest to hunt in, the American saw a land to be cleared for farms and towns.

But there *was* one area where the Indian and American saw things the same way: Each one viewed the other as being on land that *he* was meant to have. The Indian because he had been there always, and the American because he felt it was destined to be that way.

Another difference between the way Indian and American society looked at life was in the raising of children. Unlike the Plains Indians, who looked to their visions and the example of others to guide their young people, the Americans looked to education.

American children were taught, above all, respect for authority and discipline. The ideal was to try to build each child's character so that he would *want* to become a useful member of society. And if a child was unruly, instead of trying to shame him into behaving, as the Indians might do, Americans would more likely give him a rap on his knuckles.

Emmanuel, who was Pennsylvania Dutch and descended from solid German stock, was no exception to this way of thinking. With his long, flowing beard and stern expression, he even looked the part of the strict taskmaster. But his appearance was not in keeping with his nature.

To be sure, he could be strict at times. But his nature was more that of a big, playful bear. He loved to play practical jokes on his children and they, in turn, loved to play them back on him. This spirit of fun ran through the whole family and there was always someone pulling a chair from underneath someone or someone else sitting on a bent horseshoe nail.

As far as discipline went, there was almost none in the Custer household. After all, it was hard to take seriously a father who went around playing jokes on everyone like a big, overgrown kid.

In spite of all this, the children were dutiful and obeyed their parents. But it was more out of love and respect rather than a fear of punishment. The children were also bound together by this spirit of love. None of them thought of themselves as half brothers or half sisters. No one made a difference between "Pa's kids" or "Ma's kids." They were just one big, happy, joke-playing family.

Just as Crazy Horse had a nickname, so did the young boy with the curly, red hair and sparkling blue eyes. When asked to say his name, his baby attempts to say Armstrong came out "Autie." So "Autie" he was from then on.

Autie was no different from any other member of the family. He, too, loved to play practical jokes. And when the joke was on him, he laughed as hard as the prankster. It was fun to think of how he could get "even." But most of the time, *he* was the one who started the mischief. If a prank had been played, no one had to look further than Autie to get to the bottom of it.

His parents didn't mind, though. In their way of thinking, every good boy should be bad sometimes.

Autie knew that he certainly lived up to that description of a "good" boy. He also knew that he was the darling of the family and that, more times than not, he would be forgiven.

When he was four years old, Autie, like Curly,

displayed remarkable courage. One day his father took him aside and said that they would have to go to the dentist and have one of Autie's teeth pulled. Autie was deathly afraid of the dentist and for good reason. Rural dentists were not known for painless work. Also, Autie hated to see the sight of blood.

"That tooth must come out," his father said. "And if it bleeds well, it will get better right away."

Autie listened with wide eyes as his father added, "You must be a good soldier."

Emmanuel was known as one of the "good men" of the town, and was deeply religious, but he also had a militant side to him. He enjoyed belonging to the local militia, a sort of "citizens' army," and would go to each drill, taking little Autie with him. Autie soon fell in love with "playing soldier" and would go to the drills dressed smartly in a small velvet suit with big bold buttons.

So when his father told him to be a good soldier, he knew just what to do. He squared his small shoulders, puffed out his chest, and marched out of the house with his father at his side.

When they got to the dentist, Autie sat down without complaint. The dentist bent over him with a long metal forceps in his hand as Emmanuel stood by.

"Open wide now," said the doctor.

Autie dutifully opened his mouth and the pulling began. The dentist tugged and wrenched, but the tooth wouldn't come out. Then the forceps slipped and the doctor had to start all over again.

Once more came the painful tug — Autie could feel the pressure, but he didn't move. A final twist and a pull, and the tooth was free. The dentist looked at the guilty tooth in his forceps as if it were some kind of interesting bug. Then he smiled.

"That wasn't so bad, was it?" he asked.

Autie wanted to say, "It sure was!" But he just sat there and shook his head. A good soldier doesn't complain, he told himself.

On the way home, even though his jaw hurt, he jumped and skipped alongside his father as if he had just been to a fair instead of a dentist's office.

His father beamed down on him in pride.

Autie beamed back in pleasure.

"Father," he piped. "You and I can whip all the Whigs in Ohio, can't we?"

Emmanuel's long hair shook as he roared with laughter. Emmanuel was a Democrat, the political party that opposed the Whigs.

He tousled Autie's hair. It would be a good story to tell the family when they got home.

When Autie was six years old, his parents had a baby boy whom they named Tom. As soon as Tom was old enough to know what was going on, he copied his older brother in everything he did. If Autie came in from the back porch dressed like a wild Indian with a towel around his middle and a tin pot on his head, Tom would be toddling close behind with a dipper on his own curly crown. If Autie was scrambling up a tree to climb to the highest branch, little Tom would be fumbling at the trunk below trying to follow.

If Tom needed someone to show him how to be a daredevil, he couldn't have picked a better model than his older brother. Autie was a lively, daring little boy with a keen sense of adventure. And if he were still too young for real adventures, there were always rough-and-tumble games to play with his older brothers and sisters.

Wrestling, racing, fighting — Autie could never get enough to keep his restless spirit satisfied. He was a strong, handsome, and athletic lad with a happy-go-lucky nature and a wide grin.

He also had a keen musical sense, and would be forever singing a song or beating time with his feet.

The whole family shared this love of music and when they all got together, singing and tapping their hands and feet to the rhythm — including baby Tom on his high chair beating time with a spoon — the whole house seemed to tremble with the vibrations.

Emmanuel also liked music, but his interest was more in the tunes of war. He used to tell his family that as a boy he was greatly stirred by a veteran of the Revolutionary War and the War of 1812, who used to come around piping war tunes on a fife.

America was still expanding in the days when Autie was young. Just as the Indians needed warriors to protect their land and society, Americans needed soldiers to protect their expansion. So it was natural that local militia sprang up around the country so that if there was ever a call to war, Americans would be ready.

The local militia that Emmanuel belonged to was somewhat of a joke. The name, however, was grand enough. They were called the New Rumley Invincibles.

Autie, of course, didn't know the difference. To him, the New Rumley Invincibles were as fine a group of soldiers as could be seen anywhere. He was thrilled to tag along with his father. And as the men went through their drill, practicing with their guns and sabers, little Autie stood by the side with his toy gun or a stick and copied them exactly.

"A born soldier," the men said in admiration.

One day, when Autie was seven years old, he went to one of the drills with his father as usual. He had a penny flag grasped in his hand and waved it back and forth watching it flutter in the breeze.

At that time, war with Mexico loomed and there was a lot of talk about what would happen. Autie stood watching the drill and listening to the men talk about whether or not the United States would go to war with Mexico.

Suddenly little Autie waved his flag and yelled at the top of his lungs, "My voice is for war!"

The men laughed at this little boy who called for war and shook their heads in amazement. Emmanuel thought that this was so humorous that he repeated the story over and over to anyone who would listen.

Autie always seemed to say or do something that adults laughed at or admired. He began to realize that a lot of attention was paid to one who spoke and acted outrageously.

He liked the attention. It made him feel special, and he liked the feeling.

# 3
# *The Hatred Begins*

**W**hile Curly was still a young boy, the land west of the Missouri River was being settled by more and more white people. To these settlers, this was the land of opportunity, where sparkling rivers, majestic mountains, and wide-open spaces could be found in equal abundance.

To get to this bountiful country, they took a road called the Oregon Trail. It was a long and seemingly endless trail that snaked its way right into the heart of Indian territory on the Northern Great Plains.

At first, the Indians didn't mind the settlers and even lifted their hands in welcome. But the ways of the whites were new and strange and sometimes puzzling. Some of the white man's food was good, though. The strong black liquid called coffee and the sweet lumps that melted in their mouths called sugar were especially prized.

The Indians watched this ragged parade of pale-faced men, women, and children going west and wondered why they never saw when the white men came back. Surely they must be the same people going back and forth each year. There could not be that many people on all the earth!

But even though the Indians could not imagine that many people, there was room enough yet for even these numbers. The land was vast, and these people were just a little stream. But as more and more settlers came, the stream grew into a mighty river and the Indians grew uneasy. The grass was being used up by the white man's livestock, and the buffalo herds were moving away. The Indian hunters had to travel farther and farther to find fresh meat for the camps.

Now the Indians realized the true importance of what was happening. Little by little, wagon train by wagon train, the settlers were making the Indians' land their own.

The wild young men of the tribes began to grumble. "We must make war against the white man and his soldiers," they said. "It is the only way to drive him from our land and the land of our forefathers."

And the settlers answered, "These pesky savages are standing in the way of progress. They have all this land and are doing nothing with it. Why don't they just leave us alone and let us get on with our business?"

The government knew of this mounting tension and wanted to do something before any blood was shed. They proposed a peace and friendship treaty to the Indians. Government agents went out to all the tribes in the area, including Curly's. They promised the Indians presents of beads and blankets, utensils and guns, if the chiefs would come to them and "touch the pen" to a treaty paper. "Touching the pen" meant that a chief had only held a pen in his hand while a white man actually wrote down his name on the treaty.

The Indians came—riding on their spotted ponies, walking in their beaded moccasins, the feathers on their war bonnets ruffling in the prairie wind, their black hair braided or flowing free, their lances held proud and high. Shoshonis, Cheyennes, Sioux — ten thousand of them in all came to Fort Laramie in Wyoming Territory.

Fort Laramie was a government post with a small detachment of troops. It lay along the Oregon Trail to protect the emigrants that were following that road on their way westward. And it was here that the treaty was to be signed.

Curly arrived with his tribe in August of 1851 and was excited by the event. It was like one big celebration. He was thrilled to see the many different tribes. Even the Crows, one of the Sioux's longtime enemies, were there.

Fort Laramie, in the Wyoming Territory

But there was no fighting then, and the young boys spent their time playing games like racing their ponies and counting playful coups.

A coup was the act of touching a live enemy in battle. For the Indian, killing was not the purpose of war, but only one of its regrettable side effects. The Indian thought of war more as a deadly game or a dangerous sport in which he could win prestige and honors. The act of racing up to an enemy while arrows were buzzing around you, and tapping him with your spear, bow, or hand, took great daring and courage. If you were the first one to do it, it was called a first coup. If another warrior came after you and touched the same enemy, it was only a second coup for him.

A warrior could also count coup on a dead enemy if that enemy was surrounded by his own warriors. A third grade of coup was to steal a warrior's horse from under his nose. Since many warriors slept tied to their horses, it was a daring enough act to sneak up to an enemy camp, cut the rope while the warrior was sleeping, and ride away on his war pony.

A warrior who had many coups to his credit was greatly honored in his tribe, more so than one who had killed many enemies from afar with a bow and arrow or a gun. And any young man who had counted no coups was a sorry figure indeed.

Therefore it was not surprising that Curly and the other young boys spent their time playing at counting coups and dreaming of the day when they would be doing it for real. So it was that while their elders were busy signing the peace paper, the young boys were busy playing at war.

The signed treaty gave the settlers the right to use the Oregon Trail. The Indians called it the "Holy Road" now because the settlers were to be regarded as sacred things not to be bothered in any way. The Indians also promised not to make war on the white man or even each other. In return, the whites promised to give the Indians a wagon train full of goods every year. It looked as if a peaceful solution had been found, which would satisfy everyone.

But it wasn't long — only a few months later, in

fact — when the wild young Indian men who had spoken of war before were robbing, and even killing, the emigrants on the Holy Road. The emigrants were fast learning to resent the Indians who stood in the way of their westward trek, and the Indians were fast learning to resent the white men who were flooding their land like a swollen river. They blamed the white man for the disappearance of the buffalo herds from the area as well as for the new diseases, like smallpox and cholera, that he had brought with him like a deadly present.

"We can defeat the white man and blow him away like brown leaves before the wind," the young hotheads shouted to the "big bellies" — the older men.

"Those injuns need a lesson and we're just the ones to give it to 'em," grumbled the soldiers at Fort Laramie.

It wasn't long before everyone got their chance.

An argument between an Indian and a soldier at Fort Laramie ended up with the Indian shooting an arrow at the soldier. The soldiers marched out of Fort Laramie and barged into a Sioux camp and demanded the brave who had done the deed. The argument became heated, and someone fired off a shot. No one knew who did it, but suddenly the soldiers' guns boomed like thunder. When the smoke cleared, five Sioux lay dead.

A few days later, the Indians surprised a small

emigrant camp near the Fort and killed a family of four.

Now it was blood for blood, deed for deed. If an Indian was killed, a white man must die. If a white man was killed, an Indian must die.

The war of the plains had begun.

# 4
# "He Would Have Made a Pretty Girl."

At about the same time Curly was at Fort Laramie that summer, Autie was attending a county fair and having as much fun there as Curly was having at the peace meeting. He was now twelve years old and living with his half sister Lydia, and her husband, David, in a small town called Monroe, in the state of Michigan. Monroe was more worldly than New Rumley and had better schools, so his parents thought it would be best for Autie to get his education there.

David Reed had a draying business and a farm, and he owned lots of horses. So Autie, like Curly, found himself riding and learning the ways of horses at an early age.

But being at his sister's house didn't stop him

from returning to New Rumley as often as he could. In fact, he more or less divided his time between his sister's home and his parents' home.

So he soon became a well-traveled young man, at least as far as other boys of his age went. And with his sparkling blue eyes twinkling under a mop of curly blond hair, he was very popular with the girls. He was easygoing and friendly and quick to laugh. In fact, he was always laughing, always finding things to smile at, and always playing practical jokes.

Once, back in New Rumley, on a bright winter day, he decided that it was a fine day for a sleigh ride.

"Let's take some girls out for a ride," he said to his friend Joe.

Joe readily agreed. He knew that with Autie along, the prettiest girls in the area would jump at the chance.

So they hitched a team of horses to a straw-filled wagon box on runners and sped off in pursuit of the first passenger. It wasn't long before the straw-filled wagon was full of laughing rosy-cheeked girls snuggled cozily under rough, but warm, buffalo robes. Autie and Joe barely had room for themselves, but Autie kept reminding Joe of yet another girl at another farm who should be invited.

Soon the wagon was so full that Autie said to

Joe, "It seems that there's no more room for the two of us. I guess you'd better ride on one of the horses."

Before he knew what Autie was up to, Joe did just that. But as he rode uncomfortably on one of the team and looked longingly back at Autie perched cozily in the wagon, he finally realized that Autie had done it all on purpose! He figured out a way to have the last laugh, though.

"Giddup!" he yelled as he whipped the team into a fast run. The horses jerked up their heads and leaped forward with a snort. The runners of the sleigh made a loud hissing sound as they slid over the clean white snow. Faster and faster they went until they hit the first sharp turn in the road. Suddenly Autie and the laughing, screaming girls tumbled out of the wagon and into a big ditch like a bunch of rag dolls.

When Joe came back with the wagon, and saw how much everyone was laughing and had actually *enjoyed* being tumbled out, he realized that Autie had had the last laugh after all!

Even though Autie was a naturally happy-go-lucky boy, there was another side to his character. He was daring and headstrong.

Autie was a good speller and often led his class in spelling bees. During one such spelling bee in his classroom, he happened to be standing by a closed window. He was in the middle of spelling a word, when a boy classmate of his stood outside and made faces. The classmate was trying to upset him so that he would make a mistake. Without a moment's hesitation, Autie put his fist right through the window and hit the prankster square on the nose!

It seemed that the blue-eyed boy didn't give himself much time to think about things. He knew what he wanted to do and he just went ahead and did it!

In Monroe, he got a job working for one of the leading citizens, Judge Daniel S. Bacon. He would do odd jobs around the judge's yard and run little errands for the household.

The judge was a widower and had an only daughter named Libbie. She was one of the prettiest girls in town. But the judge kept a sharp eye on her and wouldn't let her socialize with anyone whom he did not think suitable. Autie, of course, being the son of a blacksmith and farmer, belonged to the "unsuitable" group.

But Autie was fascinated with Libbie from the first time he saw her. She was so pretty, so dainty, so *far* above him. He would hang around her backyard even after his jobs were done just in the hope that she might come out and say hello.

But if Autie thought about a friendship, his hopes were soon dashed by the stern image of her father looking down on him disapprovingly. He was just the Custer boy, and Libbie was the daughter of a judge.

Young
Libbie Bacon

But aside from thinking about girls, even one as pretty as Libbie, he also thought about his future. He wanted to get an education and go somewhere in the world.

He entered a school called Stebins' Academy and applied himself as best he could. But Autie soon found he was much more interested in adventure stories than he was in schoolwork.

Stories like *Charles O'Malley, Irish Dragoon,* or *Tom Burke of Ours* filled his young head with dreams of glory. Of course, this wasn't what he was supposed to be studying, so he would slip the well worn copies of the books between the covers of his schoolbooks and read them. No doubt his teacher was pleased when he saw the young Custer boy reading his schoolbooks with such an interested expression!

But in spite of all this, he did very well in most of his studies and was graduated from the Academy. He was now sixteen and fairly well educated for boys of his time. That summer, he quickly found a position as principal of a school in Harrison County, Ohio. Of course that also meant that he was the *only* teacher in the one-room schoolhouse.

Then, that winter Autie got another teaching job at a different school where part of his job was to chop wood for the school stove!

He was a popular teacher and used to play the accordion for his class at opening exercises. He still liked to wrestle, still liked to play practical jokes, and still found much to laugh at. During recess, he would tussle with the boys in the schoolyard, and wash the girls' faces with snow.

Together with his twinkling blue eyes, his red-blond hair brushed over his ears, and his ever-present smile, he was a handsome lad indeed. One of his students was so struck by his beauty that she could only think to herself, "What a pretty girl he would have made!"

# 5
# *Death of a Chief, Birth of a Dream*

**C**urly watched the smoke from the cooking pots as it curled up like wispy snakes twisting into the air. He was camped with his tribe, the Oglalas, near Fort Laramie as they waited for the goods the white man had promised would come every year after they had signed the Fort Laramie treaty. The goods that were made in that far-away land of the whites, which very few, if any, Sioux Indians had ever seen and could not even imagine.

Nearby Curly's village, the Brulés were also camped, having come to the area for the same purpose.

It was now three years since the treaty had been signed, and so far, the whites had kept their word.

In those three years, Curly had gotten a head start on Autie in learning the ways of violence. While Autie was reading about adventure, Curly was practicing it! Although he was barely a teenager and had not gone on his vision quest yet, he had already gone on raids with his younger brother, Little Hawk, and his *kola,* or great friend, Hump.

Although the chiefs had tried to live by the treaty, it was hard to control the wild young Indians in their tribes. So together with Little Hawk, Hump, and another friend called Lone Bear, Curly joined other young men as they harassed the emigrants along the Holy Road.

It was really all great sport to them — frightening the emigrants, stealing their horses and rifles, and anything else that caught their fancy. The settlers never chased them, and even if they had, they could never have caught them as they dashed away, yipping and yelling on their swift, small ponies.

So it was that an uneasy peace lay over the plains that summer. But like the haze that shimmered in the air, it was a fragile thing that could disappear at any moment.

And that moment was not long in coming, unlike the goods, which had been promised but had not yet arrived that year. The feasting and the gossiping and the celebrations were long over and still the Indians waited for the white man's presents. The children were hungry, the young men impatient. Some small emigrant trains came by, and a few wagons loaded with freight, but nothing of the promised goods.

One evening, the war that was coming like a storm began its distant rumblings with a Mormon farmer driving his footsore cow before him as he walked beside his wagon train along the Holy Road. He was passing the Brulé village when suddenly a group of boys darted out, racing their ponies. The cow bolted in fright and headed straight for the village. The cow plowed headfirst into the first tepee it came across and lumbered out the other side with a hornful of bundles. The farmer ran after his cow but, at the sight of all those Indians in the camp, he became frightened and began walking backwards like a *heyoka*, all the while shaking his club at them.

The cow blundered deep into the camp as the farmer watched helplessly. Suddenly, someone shot the cow and at that, the Mormon settler turned and ran. The women laughed to see him go over the fields like a startled jackrabbit.

The next day, the farmer stormed into Fort Laramie and demanded that the Indians pay him twenty-five dollars for his cow. "We should clean those injuns out like a nest of snakes!" he cried.

The commandant of the fort sent for Conquering Bear, who was the chief of all the Indians in the area and was camped with the Brulés. He was respected and admired by his people, but he was what was called a "white man's chief."

Indians could not imagine a chief of all the Indians. Chiefs were really men who had won their position through the years by their wisdom and by acts of daring, courage, and caring for the people. They could advise — and more often than not their advice was taken — but contrary to what the white man believed, a chief could not and would not *order* his people to do anything. But the white men needed a chief to talk for the Indians, and Conquering Bear had been chosen.

When Conquering Bear came to the Fort, the commandant, at first, was friendly. He even gave Conquering Bear and his head men bread and molasses and coffee. Then he spoke.

"I know all this fuss over a cow is foolish," he

Conquering
Bear

said. "But I am sure if you gave the owner some buffalo skins and some money, it will all be forgotten."

Conquering Bear started to talk then, but the interpreter twisted both his words and the words of the commandant, and instead of understanding each other, they ended up in an argument.

This was one of the great tragedies of American/ Indian relationships at that time. Even when people speak the same language, misunderstandings sometimes occur. But when two people have to rely on a third party to understand each other, the problem becomes multiplied. Then, too, the motives of the interpreter had to be looked at. If an interpreter disliked one person or the other, it was easy enough for him to twist the words of that person and thereby give the impression he meant one thing when he really meant another.

This was what had happened at the meeting between Conquering Bear and the commandant of Fort Laramie. The commandant got the impression that Conquering Bear was not really sincere, so he became angry and said that now it would not be enough to give buffalo robes and money for the cow. The Indian who shot it must also be brought in. Before Conquering Bear could say more, the commandant told him that the next day, ten or twelve soldiers would come to his village and arrest the man.

Conquering Bear went away with a heavy heart. It looked as if there was going to be big trouble.

The next morning a force of not ten or twelve but *thirty-one* soldiers marched out of Fort Laramie to arrest the "cow thief." They were under the command of Lieutenant John L. Grattan, a young hothead of an officer who was just itching for a fight with the Indians. Grattan had taken along two small cannons. It was as if he were ready for a big battle.

Back at the Brulé village — where by this time, Curly and most of the Oglalas had gathered — the Indians were ready for him.

They had heard of the soldiers' demand and were outraged that they had to turn over one of their own for the sake of a sick old cow! Curly watched excitedly as the warriors called in their war ponies and painted themselves for war.

He would have given anything to have been able to join them. But even though he had already killed his first buffalo, had ridden a wild horse, and was lean and strong as a young wolf, he was still too young to be a full-fledged warrior.

So he stood in an out-of-the-way place and was watchful and silent, as was becoming his way.

When Grattan and his men reached the Brulé village, they were greeted by a concerned-looking Conquering Bear. Unlike his warriors, he was not painted for war and his hair hung loose with not a single feather to adorn it. He held an old blanket around his body as he went out to meet the soldiers.

He urged Grattan to keep the soldiers out of the Indian camp. "We can smoke and sit and talk," he said, "and settle this trouble like good men."

But on top of being in a fighting mood, Grattan was also drunk. He would hear none of this, he said. He ordered his soldiers to take the cannons into the center of the village. Then he himself went and loaded the guns with grapeshot and lined them up. While this was going on, more and more warriors slipped away and hid over the bank of a nearby river.

Grattan once again demanded the surrender of the Indian who had shot the cow. Conquering Bear said he would try to see what he could do. But once again, his words were interpreted incorrectly. Now Grattan became red with anger.

"I want that man and I want him now!" he shouted.

Conquering Bear made a motion to go to his tepee, and Grattan, thinking that it was a hostile move, ordered his men to fire. Moments later, black smoke and red flames belched out of the soldiers' guns and the cannons boomed with the sound of mighty thunder. The hail of lead ripped through the tepees as if they were made of paper instead of tough buffalo hide. Conquering Bear staggered backward and crashed to the ground as if a giant hand had pushed him down.

But even before the smoke had cleared, some

warriors returned the fire and Grattan fell into a crumpled heap. Now the hidden warriors came swarming over the bank of the river, and with a great whooping, twanged their bows. The arrows flew through the air as if a great wind had blown them all at once toward the surprised soldiers. One by one they went down, moaning, screaming, and clutching the arrows that had pierced them. Then with spears and war clubs, the Indians finished off any who were still alive.

When it was over, all the soldiers, including the rash young lieutenant, lay dead like so many slain buffalo, and Conquering Bear lay mortally wounded.

Curly had witnessed the entire scene, and it had shocked him deeply. How could the white soldiers use violence for so little reason? he wondered. Why had they not listened to the peaceful words of Conquering Bear?

He was deeply disturbed and angry but had little time for thought, because already the women were starting to pull down the tepees in the Brulé camp. They must all leave or the white soldiers would come from the Fort to seek vengeance, the wise older men said.

But Curly could not control the anger he felt, and he leaped on his pony and joined other boys who were charging the now-naked bodies of the fallen soldiers.

*"Hoppo!"* They yelled out the call for charging the enemy as they raced around the bodies on

their ponies and shot off their spears and arrows as the warriors had. Then they set fire to the wooden parts of the cannon and the wagons the soldiers had brought with them, and circled the blaze, whooping and yelling and riding faster and faster, the heat of the flames matching the heat of their rage.

And when the fire was spent, so was some of Curly's anger. Together with the other Oglala boys, he spurred his pony to head back to his own village. There he found his family and tribe also getting ready to leave. His father told him that for now, they would be traveling with the Brulés instead of the Oglalas.

Day after day, Curly and his family traveled with his mother's people as they headed north and away from the scene of battle. He watched with great pity as the wounded Conquering Bear was carried along by six warriors in a buffalo hide sling. He guessed the chief was dying, but he hoped against hope that somehow it might not be so.

But one day he knew that his hopes were futile. Curly had caught a glimpse of the wounded chief as he was being lifted out of his sling. Conquering Bear's face looked so thin that the shape of his skull could be seen through the yellow-looking skin. It was the face of death. But it was a holy sign also. Curly ran to his pony and galloped off to be by himself and think about this.

When he reached a deserted spot far away from

the others, he hobbled his pony and went to lie in a gravel pit he had found. He gazed up at the blue sky.

What was he waiting for? He didn't know himself. Did he hope to have a sign from the Great Spirit to explain the things he had seen these last few days? Other thoughts crossed his brooding mind. Why was he different from the others? He did not like to talk and boast like they did. He did not like to show emotion as they did. He did not even *look* like they did.

Many times on the Holy Road, when he was younger, the settlers passing through thought that Curly might be a captive white child, so light was his hair and skin. He had become angry at that. He didn't like to think that he had anything in common with the whites.

He was Indian, he was Sioux!

All day and through that night he lay on the hard ground. He put a pile of pebbles under his back so that he wouldn't sleep. He waited and waited but nothing happened.

The next day, weak with hunger and exhaustion, he made his way back to his pony. All of a sudden, he fell to the ground in a swoon. He was about to get up when he saw a warrior on horseback pounding toward him. Where the rider had come from, he could not imagine. He had heard no sound. The warrior's horse kept changing colors before his eyes, and its hooves made no noise. Then Curly realized the horse was floating above the ground! But in his excitement at such a marvelous sight, he thought nothing of it. The warrior loomed larger, but no nearer, and Curly saw that he wore a white buckskin shirt and plain blue leggings. His face had no war paint and he wore only a single feather in the long brown hair that fell to his waist. Behind one ear a small brown stone was tied in place by a buckskin string. He didn't seem to speak, but Curly heard his words nonetheless.

"Do not wear a war bonnet. . . . Before going into battle, sprinkle gopher dust on yourself and your pony, for the tiny gopher must live by fooling his enemies. . . . Take nothing for yourself. Take no scalps. . . . If you follow this, you will never be killed by a bullet or an enemy. . . ."

All the while the man had been riding, streaks of lead balls and arrows had been flashing toward him, aimed by a shadowy enemy. But before they could strike the phantom rider, they disappeared. Then other shadows grabbed at him — Curly sensed they were the warrior's own people — and tried to hold him back. But he shrugged them off and rode on. A thunderstorm sprang up then and swirled around the rider. And as if in answer to the bolts of lightning that zigzagged across the heavens, a painted red lightning flash appeared on his cheek.

Now Curly saw that the warrior was naked, except for a breechcloth, and white hail spots from the storm decorated his body. Curly watched in wonder as the vision continued.

Shadows again reached out to grab at the warrior, and again the warrior broke free from their grasp. But the storm was fading and the figure with it.

The shadow people started to make a great noise, and a red-backed hawk, which had suddenly appeared over the warrior's head, added its screech to the clamor. Then the storm, the shadow people, and the warrior disappeared, and Curly found himself alone once more.

His head reeled with amazement. Had it only been a dream after all? A dream brought on by his hunger and exhaustion? But it hadn't seemed like a dream. And the rider had seemed familiar. He had been slim and had had long brown hair like himself. Could it be? Were that warrior and he the same person? Had he seen his future?

Somehow Curly knew it must be so. And he also knew deep in his heart that it couldn't have been a dream. He knew that at last, he had gotten his vision!

He lay back thinking about this and soon fell into a deep sleep. He awoke to find his father and Hump — who was also with the Brulés — standing over him. His father was angry. Curly had left the village without telling anyone where he was going.

"I came to seek a vision, Father," he said.

At that, his father grew angrier still. "How do you dare to seek a vision when you have not prepared yourself properly?" he cried. "When you have not purified yourself or sought advice from the Wise Ones for guidance!"

Curly was so chastened by his father's words that at the moment he didn't dare tell him that he *had* had a vision. So he just followed his father and Hump to the village without saying a word.

A few days later, Conquering Bear died. Even as Curly's heart was glad about his vision, it now hardened against the whites. So this was what came of trying to talk peace with the white man!

# 6
## A Lovely Girl
## or a Lovely Uniform?

If Autie thought about the plains at all — where Curly was even now tasting the bitter fruits of war — it was as a far-off, romantic place full of adventure. If he thought about Indians, it was also in that same vein. As yet, he had not met any wild Indians, but he fancied them as noble savages living a free, natural life. He even admired them for their courage and daring.

His main thoughts right now, however, were his plans for the future. He wanted to get a better education, but his family didn't have the money for any more schooling. The military academy of West Point, however, was free, and besides, the life of a soldier now appealed to him. Like Curly, he, too, wanted to be admired and respected.

What better way than as an officer and a gentleman?

But there were two things standing in the sixteen-year-old teacher's way. The first was, in order to go to West Point, you had to be appointed by a local congressman — in this case, a man named John A. Bingham. The second was that he had fallen in love!

As a teacher, he had moved away from his family and he needed a place to live. He found a room in the home of a well-to-do farmer. The farmer's daughter was named Mary Holland and she was almost as pretty as Libbie Bacon. Maybe prettier, because, as Autie found out, love always makes the object of one's affection more attractive.

And Mary seemed to return that affection, since Autie was soon writing love letters and poems as fast as he could compose them. Poems like:

**To Mary**
I've seen and kissed that crimson lip
With honied smiles o'erflowing.
Enchanted watched the opening rose,
Upon thy soft cheek glowing.
Dear Mary, thy eyes may prove less blue,
Thy beauty fade tomorrow.
But Oh, my heart can ne'er forget
Thy parting look of sorrow.

One can only wonder if Mary's father knew about kissing that "crimson lip." In any case, like

48

Custer before
he went to
West Point, holding
a picture of the
girl he left behind

Judge Bacon, the wealthy farmer did not consider Autie a suitable husband for his daughter. So, knowing of his desire to go to West Point, and knowing that cadets couldn't marry, he lost no time in convincing Congressman Bingham that Autie would make a fine soldier.

Now Autie had a clear-cut choice. He was serious about Mary to the point where he was thinking of marriage. But he was also serious about his career.

Being practical, he realized that winning Mary would be a long, uphill battle with no certain victory at the end. On the other hand, West Point was there for the taking. With his customary swiftness of decision, he choose West Point. He had not given up the idea of marrying Mary, though. He just postponed it. He reasoned that once he became an officer, Mary's father might take more kindly to him as a possible son-in-law.

The paddlewheels of the steamboat carrying Autie and a group of other boys slapped into the waters of the Hudson River as the boat made its way down the wide, traffic-clogged river to the West Point dock.

On the way, Autie saw more boats than he had ever seen in his life. Steamboats, barges, sailboats, canalboats — all glided past his wondering eyes. And if he had any ideas of how sailors went about the daily routine of living on the water, he soon found out it was nothing like he had imagined. Clotheslines, stretched between masts, held shirts, towels, underwear, and an assortment of unidentified garments that fluttered in the breeze like ragtag flags.

Garbage was thrown over the side in careless fashion, sinking as it hit the water, but sometimes bobbing behind in the wake as soggy evidence of a boat's passing.

Autie mingled with the other passengers. As always, he soon made friends with his easygoing ways and great sense of humor. At this time, he was of about average height and, like Curly, slim and agile. His actions were quick and his eyes darted from side to side above a long pointed nose, looking for all the world as if he were expecting someone to play a trick on him at any moment. Or, for that matter, like someone looking to play a trick on someone else!

Although he was well built and had sharp, well defined features, a lot of his attraction came from his coloring. A healthy, ruddy complexion, wavy, red-blond hair, blue eyes, and even white teeth all combined to make the young Custer a splendid-looking young man.

There were also other fine-looking young men on the boat heading for West Point, and through the journey, they and Autie had joked, played, and wondered what was waiting for them at the academy.

Their wondering was soon to be over, for the boat was fast approaching the West Point dock.

The steamboat's paddle wheels began to churn the water as it drifted toward the pier. Autie could see a sloping mountainside in front of him. Then he noticed a shelf — the famous Academy Plain — and towering above the shelf was an American flag fluttering in the breeze like a patriotic beacon.

Custer had arrived!

# 7
# *"I Call Him Crazy Horse!"*

**W**hile Custer was learning the ways of war through books, Curly was already practicing them through deeds. It was now four years since Conquering Bear's death and the Grattan Massacre, as the whites called it, and Curly had seen enough of the white man's treachery and violence to convince him that the best thing for the Indian to do would be to keep away from him and live the good, wild life as his forefathers had done.

He was well on his way to being the man in his vision. He had gone on many raids and had even killed the enemy. He was truly a young warrior now.

At about the same time that Autie was at West Point, living the strict and sometimes boring life of a cadet, Curly was riding over the plains, living the free, and sometimes violent, life of an Indian brave.

In the summer of 1858, Curly joined Hump, Little Hawk, Lone Bear, and other young warriors on a war party headed west toward the Wind River in Wyoming. It was the farthest west that any Oglala Sioux had previously traveled.

They were out to raid a tribe of Arapaho Indians that were said to be relatives of the Shoshonis, or Snakes. The tribe spoke a different language and little was really known of them. But the different-tongued Indians were said to have very good horses, and it was these that the raiding party was after.

Later photographs of Crazy Horse's brother Little Hawk (left), and his *kola* Hump

Curly prepared himself for battle as he had done ever since he had had his vision. He painted a red zigzag line that ran from the top of his forehead, down one side of his nose, and on to the base of his chin. A single hawk feather decorated his long brown hair, and a small brown stone was tied in place behind one ear. He dabbed yellow spots on his body to resemble hail, and when he had done that, he went to get some gopher dust to sprinkle on his body and on his war pony.

Now his medicine was good. Now he knew that no bullet would find him, no arrow would pierce him.

When the others in the war party were ready, they spurred their ponies and headed for the land of the strange Indians. But the Arapahoes had known of their coming and were waiting for them on the high ground of a hill, long before the Sioux war party had reached the village.

But the Sioux had not come this far to be turned back so easily.

"We will make a circling," Hump told the others. Then with a whoop and a yell, he led the others in a circle around the Arapahoes.

Arrows and bullets sliced through the air seeking their human targets as Curly hugged his horse and shot his bow from under its neck. A cloud of dust was churned up by the circling Sioux as they tried to pry their foes off the hilltop. But the Arapahoes held firm.

For two hours the battle went on with no winner. Then Curly's horse went down and the young warrior tumbled and rolled onto the ground. As he jumped to his feet, a wild Arapaho pony came galloping toward him. With the agility of a mountain lion he sprang onto its back and whirled around to join his comrades. But the wild young horse was startled by the shot of a gun and instead of obeying Curly's commands, it leaped ahead, straight for the enemy hill!

"*Hoka-hey!*" yelled Curly. "So be it!"

Curly charged the hill as light and safe as the warrior in his vision. He could hear arrows and bullets whizzing past, filling the air around him with an angry hum. But, as had happened in his vision, they seemed to melt away and none struck him.

As he thundered onto the hill, he counted one coup after the other, touching the enemy with his bow even as they tried to kill him. He counted three coups in all before he jerked his horse around and retreated with a whoop and a holler. He could hear the bows of the enemy twanging as they shot their arrows at his back. But again nothing hit him.

His friends yelled out his name again and again in honor of his bravery as he galloped toward them. "Curly! Curly!"

His heart swelled with pride and he grinned through the dust and dirt and the sweat-streaked war paint on his face. As he reached his comrades, he suddenly whirled his pony around and again raced up the hill.

"No," called Hump. "You have done enough!" But the song of battle was singing in his heart and he couldn't stop himself even if he had wanted to.

This time, as he dashed for the hill, a brave Arapaho leaped from a gully and aimed his gun point-blank at the headstrong youth. Curly slotted an arrow into his bow, and timing his shot to the steady rhythm of his galloping pony, he twanged it off straight at the Arapaho. The man went down with a cry and lay still. But another warrior appeared out of nowhere and took his place. Curly leaped his pony over the dead man, whirled, and again shot his bow. The arrow found its mark with a "swis-s-sh!" and the second warrior lay dead.

Curly was hot with the heat of battle, and he leaped off his horse to take the scalps of the dead men. Bullets kicked pieces of earth and pebbles into his face and arrows appeared like magic in the ground around him with a "Twunk! Twunk!" sound.

But in spite of this, Curly cut off the scalps and was about to mount his pony when an arrow sliced into his leg. The wild horse jerked loose, and Curly was left to flee down the hill on foot. He jumped this way and that so that the enemy would not know where to aim, and finally made it back to Hump and the other warriors.

Only when he was back among his own people did he remember his vision. He was not to take scalps! That was why he had been wounded, he was sure. So he threw away the bloody scalps and watched as Hump cut the arrowhead from his leg and dressed the wound with a fresh piece of skin from a dead horse. "It is enough for today," Hump said. "We will go back to our village now."

Hump picked up the scalps that Curly had thrown away and looped them under his belt. Then the war party headed back to their village, leaving the Arapahoes on the hill to mourn their dead.

Before the Sioux war party reached their village, Hump sent a warrior ahead to announce their safe return. Then the war party came in, spears bright in the sun, war bonnets bending with the wind, and shields held high. And in back rode Curly, nursing his wounded leg, but holding his head up high.

There was a big victory dance that night and Curly was twice pushed forward into the circle and told to sing a song in praise of his deeds. But the light-skinned, light-haired boy would not, and each time he was pushed into the circle, he backed out.

Here indeed was a strange Indian, the people thought, because it was almost unheard of for a Sioux warrior not to boast of his deeds. But still, the people looked at this boy with new interest and wonder. He was small yet for a warrior, but his deeds were big. He was one to watch.

But it was Curly who was watching the others that night. He did not speak because that was not his way and besides, he had a lot to think about. Why did he forget about not taking scalps? What good was it to have a vision if you forgot its instructions in the first fight?

He went to sleep that night with these things on his mind.

The next morning when he awoke, Curly still felt badly about going against his vision, so he lay in his family's lodge, not moving or speaking. His brother, Little Hawk, thought he was still asleep, so he and the rest of the family quietly left the tepee. After a while, Curly did fall asleep again and it wasn't until the sun was directly overhead that he awoke.

Then his father, Crazy Horse, came into the lodge and took his ceremonial blanket from its case. The blanket had a beaded band across the middle showing all the things that his father had seen in his visions.

"What is happening?" asked Curly as he sat up. "Why are you taking your sacred blanket?"

But instead of answering, his father left the tepee and wrapped the blanket around himself. Then he went through the whole village singing a song that he had made up. He sang loudly so that all the people might hear:

> My son has been against the people of
>   unknown tongue.
> He has done a brave thing —
> For this I give him a new name, the name
>   of his father, and of many fathers
>   before him —
> I give him a great name
> I call him Crazy Horse.

Curly heard his father's song and was thunderstruck. He did not expect such an honor as this!

Then all the people of the village who wanted to honor the brave young man followed his father back to his lodge where Curly still sat. Young and old, men and women, they all came to sing the praises of the young new warrior among them. The young new warrior whom everybody believed was destined for greatness. The young new warrior with the great name of Crazy Horse!

# 8
# Promotions or a Coffin!

**W**est Point was known for turning out fine, disciplined soldiers — the cream of the officer corps. But if Custer was going to turn into one of these splendid young officers, he certainly gave no hint of it his first years there.

He was a sloppy soldier. His uniform was frequently out of order, his equipment dirty, and his drills slack. It seemed as if he had forgotten the way he had drilled so smartly at his father's side with the New Rumley Invincibles. He was called Armstrong now, but in a lot of ways, he was still little Autie — taking nothing really seriously, always looking for a good time, always playing practical jokes. Even in the classroom his fun-loving nature was hard to repress.

Once during French class, Custer was asked to translate: *Leopold, duc d'Autriche, se mettit sur les plaines*. The first part of the translation should have been: *Leopold, Duke of Austria*. But Custer began the translation by saying: "Leopard, duck, and ostrich . . ."

His classmates chuckled so much that the rest of the translation was lost in laughter.

Another time, in Spanish class, Custer cut in on his instructor and asked him how one would say "Class is dismissed" in Spanish. The teacher promptly told him, and with that, Custer marched himself and the rest of the class out of the classroom!

But even though his behavior was undisciplined in many ways, he knew just how much he could get away with, and he never went over that line. When he had to study he studied, and when he had to behave he behaved.

Maybe one of the reasons that Custer was so intent on having some fun was that West Point was so intent on not allowing him to.

Cadets were forbidden — among other things — to drink liquor, play cards, go off the post, swim in the river, and play a musical instrument. Instead, they had to eat inferior food, live in cold rooms in winter, get along with no recreation, and wear uncomfortable uniforms.

Custer's uniform, like his fellow cadets', was ill-fitting and too tight. The coat, especially, was so uncomfortable that the cadets had a verse for it:

Your coat is made,
you button it,
give one spasmodic cough,
And do not draw another breath
until you take it off!

Even though the uniform was supposed to make a cadet look like a manly soldier, Custer still looked very much like a boy with his narrow face and long curly locks, which he now brushed back with the help of cinnamon-scented hair oil.

And "Cinnamon," as he was soon nicknamed, could always be counted on to lighten the sometimes dreary days of study, work, and drills.

But with all this, Custer loved the Point and would not have left it for the world. He felt he was getting a good education there and he even wrote his sister, Ann, a letter stating, ". . . I would not leave this place for any amount of money, for I would rather have a good education and no money than a fortune and be ignorant."

In his recreational reading however, he still liked novels full of romance and adventure. One of the first books he took out of the Academy library was named *Swallow Barn*. It was a story of the old South and its hero was a young man named Ned Hazard. Ned went around on his horse, followed by a pack of hounds, and was a dashing and adventurous type who was popular with the girls. Like Custer, Ned had troubles with his studies, too, so it wasn't hard to imagine that Custer saw a lot of himself in Ned.

He also liked to read books about the wilds of America, like *The Last of the Mohicans,* and *The Deerslayer.* Books that told of hardy men who hunted and rode and fought Indians in the wilderness. These stories appealed to Custer's romantic side and he probably thought there was no better way to live than to be in one daring and dangerous adventure after the other, as were the buckskinned-clad heroes in his favorite books.

At the Point, the adventures were not dangerous — at least not in the real sense of the word — but they could be daring due to the fact that too bold an act could lead to expulsion. But still, Custer found it hard to control his fun-loving spirit. Talking in ranks, playing cards, and throwing snowballs at other cadets on parade were temptations he found hard to resist.

But if he found it hard to pay attention to his schoolbooks, he found it easier to apply himself to the physical skills required at the Point, especially horsemanship.

Like Crazy Horse, he had been riding horses almost before he had learned how to walk. He could even ride bareback like an Indian. Custer soon showed the other cadets how well he could jump a three-foot hurdle while slashing at a

Custer as a young cadet

stuffed leather head with his saber. In fact, he was one of the best and highest jumpers at the Academy.

Again, though, if he was a superb horseman, he was a poor student of cavalry tactics and received low grades in that vital study. He also got low grades in English, although he still loved to write. In fact, one of the essays he was most pleased with was one called *The Red Man*. It was a very sympathetic portrait of the Indian, but as one can imagine, most of his knowledge came from the novels he had read and not from firsthand experience.

Custer spent four years at West Point, and during that time, he dropped the idea of marrying Mary Holland. It seemed that he had fallen out of love with her and in love with the army. Although he had fond memories of her — as she surely had of him — he just wanted to be a soldier now more than anything else.

The years at the Point made him realize that he was ideally suited for the military life. He still loved music but now he marched to the beat of military tunes. In spite of the fact that he was a bit sloppy, it seemed as if the militiamen who had marveled at the little boy in blue who drilled alongside them so long ago were right. Little Autie Custer was indeed a "born soldier."

Custer was due to graduate in 1862, but in 1861 the Civil War broke out and the army needed officers. So Custer's class was moved up one year and graduated in June of 1861. Custer had squeaked through, but just barely. At graduation, he was at the bottom of his class.

When he went up to get his diploma, he bowed solemnly as his classmates cheered wildly. The curly-haired prankster with the wide grin and happy-go-lucky nature had made it! He and his other classmates were now officers in the United States Army.

With graduation behind them, Custer and his fellow officers were now eager to get into the war. It seemed to Custer that this was what he had been looking for all along. War suited his personality. There he could make good use of his daring, courageous, and headstrong ways.

". . . It is useless to hope the coming struggle will be bloodless or of short duration," he wrote to his sister Ann. "Much blood will be spilled and thousands of lives, at the least, lost. If it is to be my lot to fall in the service of my country and my country's rights, I will have no regrets."

So Custer prepared himself for war.

It was a well-known fact that promotions in wartime were much faster than in peacetime. That was, of course, if one lived long enough to be promoted. The cadets had their own way of putting it: "Promotions or a coffin!"

# 9
## *"The Boy General with the Golden Locks"*

**I**f Custer was impatient to get into the fight, he didn't have very long to wait. The very same summer that he graduated, he found himself a Union officer in the first battle of the war.

The Confederate and Union armies were fighting at a place called Bull Run in Virginia, and Custer was with his unit, the Second Cavalry, waiting for orders.

July 21, 1861, the morning of the battle, had dawned with a pale, milky light in the east that foretold a hot day, and the promise had been fulfilled. Together with the heat and the tension of waiting, Custer and his men were perspiring freely as they sat on their horses, waiting to get into the fight.

With Custer was another young officer named

Lieutenant Walker. Custer saw the Lieutenant's hands shake as he fixed the bridle on his horse. Custer was scared and nervous, too. Even though he had imagined what a battle would be like, this was his first experience with the real thing.

Soon the orders came for the Second Cavalry to move up and deploy itself in a small valley nearby. Their job was to protect some Union artillery that had been placed on the hill above them. Custer waited with Walker and the Second Cavalry in a small hollow in case the Rebels decided to attack the guns. He could hear the loud "sw-o-osh!" of shells as they hissed overhead, and he could see the little puffs of cottony clouds as they exploded in the blue sky.

Soon the cry came: "The Rebels are massing on the other side of the hill!"

The order to advance was given and the Second Cavalry moved out. This was it!

Custer was at the head of one platoon and Walker was at the head of another. Young Walker was an officer plucked right out of civilian life and had no experience with a real charge. The nervous young man yelled across to him. "Custer, what weapon are you going to use in the charge?"

Even though it was Custer's first time, too, he answered firmly as a West Pointer was taught to do. "The saber!" he called out as he drew his blade.

Lieutenant Walker drew his own and the line moved slowly forward. A few seconds later, Custer changed his mind about the saber. He put back his sword and unbuckled his revolver holster. He glanced at Walker and saw him do the same. As the horses walked up the hill toward the guns, he changed his mind again and drew his saber. Walker did the same.

If Custer needed anything to calm him down, this was it. Even though he really *wasn't* sure of which weapon to use, he immediately saw how funny the situation was. Even in the midst of danger, his joke-loving nature couldn't be repressed. So he put his saber back and again put his hand at the ready by his revolver.

Walker did the same.

Custer was so amused by this that he repeated the act several times and by the time the troopers got to the top of the hill, ready to charge down on the Rebels, Custer had forgotten his own fears.

But this time there was no need to be anxious because the Rebels weren't attacking the line of guns after all. So Custer and Walker withdrew their men and once again waited for orders.

Custer was to learn that waiting was a big part of war, but he never learned to accept it. He was impatient and always eager for action. Waiting was for thinkers, not doers, and Custer was a doer. He proved that in other action that day, and even though the fight had ended up with the Union Army retreating, he was cited for bravery.

All through the war Custer seemed to be doing daring and courageous things while others were watching. Although there are many acts of bravery in war, a great number of times there is no one to see them, least of all an officer. But Custer always seemed to be in the right place at the right time.

Time and again Custer proved his courage and daring. He was a reckless and seemingly fearless leader. And most of all, he loved to lead a charge.

In another one of his first battles, he and his command were approaching a hill where a Rebel unit was sniping at them from the crest.

Bullets twanged overhead like the strings of a gigantic guitar. But the enemy couldn't be seen from where Custer was. Without a moment's hesitation, Custer decided to charge the hill.

They started off slowly at first. The enemy was hidden, but the Rebel bullets buzzing through the air proved that they were there.

When the troopers were close to the summit, Custer turned to his men and yelled, "Draw sabers! Charge!" as he whipped out his own gleaming blade from its scabbard.

The cavalry thundered up the hill and the force of their charge carried them over the crest. Custer held his saber high, ready to slash anyone he found in his way. He expected to find the enemy in full force behind the ridge. But the Rebels had retreated and were now scurrying over the countryside and popping off shots behind them.

Custer smiled. There had been no fight but he was no less excited. It had been the first time in his life that he had given the command to charge, and the memory of his men dashing forward with him, their sabers gleaming in deadly beauty, their horses galloping fiercely, made him feel very proud. And on top of that, it had been fun!

Another time he was with a general and a group of his officers. They had come to a wide river and the general wondered if his army could cross it. "I wish I knew how deep it is," said the general.

No one moved, but suddenly Custer spurred his horse and plunged right into the flowing water. He and his horse quickly reached the other bank without sinking, and then he turned around and came back across. "That's how deep it is, General," Armstrong Custer said with a small grin.

This act took more courage on Custer's part than might be imagined. First, he really didn't know if he and his horse would have to end up swimming and perhaps sinking in the cold waters. Secondly, he had an intense fear of water.

But the daring act proved worthwhile because the general promptly said, "Do you know, you're just the young man I've been looking for, Mr. Custer." And he immediately offered Armstrong a position on his staff. Not only that, the position came with a promotion to captain! "Promotions or a coffin!" was being played out.

During the war, Custer seemed to be everywhere at once. He was even sent aloft in a hot-air balloon a number of times to spy on enemy positions. Again, this was no small feat for Custer.

He had made up his mind that he might be killed by a bullet, a saber slash, or an exploding shell. That was part of the war he knew. But to be sent hundreds of feet into the air in a fragile basket with a flimsy-looking balloon puffed up with hot air above him more than tested his courage.

And so it was, all through the war. He had had horses shot out from under him, bullets clip his uniform and equipment, men fall around him, but like Crazy Horse, he seemed to ride through them all safely. Like Crazy Horse, Custer seemed to be incredibly lucky in battle. "Custer's Luck," his men began to call it.

And like Crazy Horse, he actually enjoyed combat. So even though he and Crazy Horse were as different from each other as could be, as far as race and upbringing went, they certainly shared one thing in common. Each one looked at war as one big game where one had only one's life to lose — but glory and honors to gain.

Custer wrote to a friend, ". . . Oh, could you but have seen some of the charges that were made! While thinking of them I cannot but exclaim 'Glorious War!' "

Those glories and honors came fast and furious for the young firebrand officer. At the age of twenty-three he was made a brigadier general! Now he had thousands of men under his command.

Custer around
the time of
the Civil War

General Custer!

The grimly laughing, devil-may-care Armstrong did not look much like the little curly-haired Autie with twinkling blue eyes in a face that might have made a pretty girl. But that little boy still dwelled close to the surface, ready to pop out at a moment's notice.

It was the little boy who had gone to look for his orderly with his promotion papers in his hand, and when he found him, shyly said, "I have been made a brigadier general."

"The deuce you have!" said the orderly, surprised and pleased himself.

Then Custer looked around as if looking for a

lost button. He grinned self-consciously. "How am I going to get something to show my rank?" he asked.

The orderly told him that he would try to find some stars. The next morning, the orderly came to Custer with two bright stars in his hand. Custer handed him his uniform jacket and the orderly sewed a star on each corner of the collar. Custer put on the jacket and wrapped a red tie around his neck.

It wasn't long before he adopted a new uniform, though, one that little Autie would have happily approved of. He wore a velveteen jacket with five gold loops on each sleeve, and a sailor shirt with a very large collar. The shirt was dark blue, and with it, he wore a blazing red tie. He topped everything off with a soft, wide hat from which his red-blond curls flowed almost down to his shoulders.

"The Boy General with the Golden Locks," he was called.

# 10
# *The Violent Plains*

**A**ll through the years that Custer had been at West Point and in the Civil War, Crazy Horse had been growing into a great warrior. He was not known in civilized society as Custer was, but to his own people he was just as famous.

It was now the spring of 1866, and Crazy Horse was about 24 years old. Like Custer, he had risen quickly in the ranks of his people and was now a "Shirt Wearer." To be a Shirt Wearer was a great honor given to one who had proven himself a great warrior and a protector of his people.

It was not the same as being a brigadier general as Custer was, although it would be hard to compare the two ranks since the white man and the Indian had vastly different views of what made up honor and prestige.

One of Crazy Horse's dress shirts. No photo of Crazy Horse was ever taken of him, because he believed it was bad luck.

The title "Shirt Wearer," naturally enough, was given because the chosen one would be awarded a special shirt to wear. Besides Crazy Horse, there were only three other Shirt Wearers in the whole tribe.

The shirts themselves were lovingly and carefully made of bighorn sheepskin with the dew claws left on. The skin of the forelegs formed the sleeves, and across the shoulders and along the arms were bands of pictures of men, horses, and weapons. The sleeves were fringed with scalp hair, each lock in memory of a great deed done by the wearer. There were over two hundred forty such locks on Crazy Horse's shirt! From then on, it would be a constant reminder to all of his skill and bravery.

The Indians needed brave young leaders now more than ever. The war that had begun with the fight at Conquering Bear's village had been simmering on and off through the years. It was perhaps less a war than a series of skirmishes between whites and Indians, like the quick, violent thunderstorms that erupted on the plains in a burst of noise and lightning and then were gone. Even so, there was enough violence between whites and Indians to justify calling it a war.

It was a war, however, with no clear-cut enemy — at least on the part of the whites. The Indian who was trading with you one day might very well be the Indian who had attacked a wagon train the day before. It was hard to fight a war if you weren't sure who the villain was.

This also led to one of the great tragedies of the conflict. Sometimes soldiers would attack a peaceful village in the belief that it was hostile. Inhuman acts were often performed during those attacks. Scalping and mutilation were not restricted to the Indians. Many white soldiers had picked up the gruesome practice, too.

The typical soldiers at that time were a rough, devil-may-care lot. Many of them were criminals who had joined the army one jump ahead of the law. Others were men who just wanted to get to the West and felt the army was a free ticket there. Many were misfits and drunks. It didn't take much to arouse horrible brutality among the worst of these soldiers.

Sometimes troopers, under the command of a drunken or glory-seeking officer — and drunk themselves, for that matter — attacked villages, not caring very much whether they were hostile or not. To these men, *all* the Indians were fair game. "A good Indian is a dead Indian," was a favorite saying of this type of soldier.

It made no difference anymore who had started it all. The Indians would attack a white settlement and then the soldiers would strike back in revenge. The soldiers would attack an Indian village and the Indians would strike back in revenge. And so the violence on the plains went on.

But this is not to say that there weren't many

peace-loving Indians and peace-loving whites on the plains. For the most part, the battles were fought between the army and young warriors like Crazy Horse and other Indians who were bent on resisting the white invasion of their lands.

Then in 1862 something happened that speeded up the invasion even more. Gold was discovered in southwestern Montana and a parade of new emigrants had begun to once again tramp on Indian soil. Unlike the emigrants on the Holy Road, however, this time they weren't looking for golden opportunities but for gold itself!

The path that they traveled was called the Bozeman Trail and like the Holy Road, it, too, cut through Indian land — the land that had been promised to them by the Laramie treaty, the very same treaty that had been signed when Crazy Horse was a young boy.

At first, the Indians had let the miners travel this road in relative peace. The warriors were more interested in fighting other tribes and the soldiers from the forts than in bothering a relatively few white prospectors.

Crazy Horse and the other Sioux warriors were now under the leadership of a warrior chief called Red Cloud. Red Cloud was the "general" who planned the overall strategy for the Indian's long-standing campaign against the whites, and Crazy Horse was his "field commander" who oversaw the day-to-day fighting.

Like Custer, his fame grew day by day. But

Crazy Horse knew that the time was fast approaching when the white man and Indian must fight a final war for possession of the plains.

And he had seen enough of the white man's military tactics to realize that the Indians must fight as a unit, the way the whites did. This was not a game anymore, as the Indians had thought of war. The white soldier fought to kill, not to play. He had no desire to count coups on a live enemy. The only way a soldier wanted to touch his enemy was in death! The Indian must learn this lesson from the white man or perish.

So in this spring of 1866, as the air warmed up and flowers began once more to bud on the northern Great Plains, the red-white crisis slowly started to head toward a climax.

Crazy Horse and the other hostiles were determined to keep the white man out of the Powder River Country in Wyoming and Montana Territories, where the Bozeman Trail ran. The white man, on the other hand, was determined to forge ahead — Indians or no Indians. The Civil War was over and the government could now turn its full attention to expanding the country. And one of the main obstacles left to this dream was the Powder River Sioux.

The government tried to buy its way into the territory by promising the Indians well-located reservations, plus food and money on a yearly basis. But as far as Crazy Horse was concerned, nothing the white man offered would justify giving up the land.

Even as the government was talking of treaties, it sent a small detachment of soldiers under the command of a Colonel Carrington into Sioux territory. They had orders to build forts along the Bozeman Trail so that the army could protect white travelers.

In spite of this, the government called for a council at Fort Laramie. They especially wanted the hostile Indians to "touch the pen" on a new treaty.

Red Cloud came to the council along with some older chiefs, but Crazy Horse stayed away. Red Cloud had come mostly to hear what the whites had to offer. A man from the Indian Office named Taylor talked to them. He said that the United States government only wanted to insure that the white man had the right to use the Bozeman Trail. But he did not tell them that the government already had sent soldiers to build forts along its route.

Taylor had promised the Indians money and goods, and guns for hunting. Red Cloud and the other chiefs were thinking about signing the treaty. Maybe it would be a good thing for their people after all. But just as they were about to touch the pen, a chief named Standing Elk galloped into Fort Laramie with the news that he had met Carrington and his soldiers and was told that they were going to build forts along the Bozeman Trail.

Red Cloud faced Taylor and the other white men in the council and angrily said, "The Great Father sends us presents and wants us to sell him the road, but White Chief goes with soldiers to steal the road before Indians say yes or no." With that, he stormed out of the council tent, followed by the other chiefs.

But in spite of Red Cloud's angry outburst and the knowledge that the Indians resented it, the army went ahead with its plans. Carrington built a fort named Fort Kearny and another called Fort C.F. Smith along the Bozeman Trail.

Red Cloud, the great warrior chief, under whom Crazy Horse fought

If he expected a reaction from Red Cloud, he was not disappointed. Within a week after Fort Kearny was operational, Red Cloud set up his own camp along the Powder River, which was in striking distance of the fort. He also assembled a great army of Indians made up of Oglala Sioux, Sans Arcs, and Northern Cheyenne, among others. Each day, his warriors would go out to waylay and kill any travelers who had ventured out of the fort onto the Bozeman Trail. The gold-seekers were soon to realize that the price of gold could be their lives.

Crazy Horse was one of Red Cloud's chief warriors in this siege of Fort Kearny, and hardly a day went by when he wasn't leading a war party to harass the whites along the Bozeman Trail. If the Oregon Trail was called the Holy Road, this winding road through the wilderness could now be called the *un*holy road, littered as it was with the wrecks of burned wagons and the bodies of dead horses and scalped whites.

Red Cloud and Crazy Horse knew that Fort Kearny itself was too strong to attack, but it did have a weakness. The only stand of woods was five miles or so from the fort. Every time the men needed wood for fuel and construction, they had to go out to these trees and cut some down.

It was these woodcutting parties that Crazy Horse and his warriors attacked at every opportunity. And every time a woodcutter's party was attacked, the soldiers would pour out of the fort and pursue the attackers, usually with no success, for the Indians would melt into the countryside before their eyes.

In the meantime, more and more warriors clustered to Red Cloud's camp. It would be just a matter of time before they would have enough to take on the soldiers in an all-out battle.

Red Cloud and Crazy Horse didn't mind waiting.

# 11
# *Love, Marriage, and Indians*

That same year of 1866, while Crazy Horse was riding the wild prairies of the plains, Custer was walking the civilized streets of Monroe. The Civil War had ended in 1865 and he had come out of it a national hero. Newspapers and popular magazines had been full of his war adventures. And no wonder — he was a reporter's dream. He was handsome and dashing and brave. No one could ask for a more likely subject to idolize.

Everywhere he went, people noticed him and wanted to shake his hand. It was flattering and exciting, but it was nothing compared to the thrill and excitement he had felt in the war. But if he was restless, he was also happy. He now was married to the girl of his dreams — Libbie Bacon!

Although they had known each other by sight when they were both children, when Custer had been doing odd jobs for her father, they had never really been introduced. But after Custer became a Civil War hero, he was invited to the Bacon household as an honored guest.

The first time he went, it was Thanksgiving day. It was then that he was properly introduced to the dark-haired, ivory-skinned beauty that he had so admired from afar as a young man.

With customary swiftness, he started courting her right after that meeting. At first, her father objected to the courtship. After all, he wanted the best for his daughter, and he wasn't sure this young firebrand of a soldier would make a good husband. But if the truth be known, he was only acting like any other father, who thinks that no one is ever good enough for his daughter.

But in the end, Libbie's father consented to the match. Resisting their marriage was like trying to resist a whirlwind. Libbie was hopelessly in love with the dashing young officer and he with her. Also, he was now a national hero and to think he was unsuitable almost seemed unpatriotic!

The ceremony took place in Monroe, Ohio on February 9, 1864, and it was a grand affair. The bride wore a mint-green hoop-skirted wedding dress with long sleeves, and the groom was decked out in full-dress uniform — his hair brushed back and gleaming and smelling pleasantly of cinnamon oil. They looked like a wedding-cake couple.

Two years later Libbie's father died, and the couple found themselves back in Monroe to attend the funeral. It was there that Custer learned he would be given a command on the western frontier with the rank of lieutenant colonel.

When Libbie heard the news, she accepted it with good grace. Although the frontier promised rough living and unknown dangers, wherever her husband went, she would go. There was never any question about it.

Custer was to take command of the new Seventh Cavalry, which was being organized at Fort Riley, Kansas. Experienced officers were needed to combat the increasing number of hostile Indians on the central and southern plains, who were killing white settlers and torturing anyone unlucky enough to fall into their hands.

To Custer, the command was a step down. After all, it was hard to be a colonel after being a general. The rank of general, however, was a temporary one given to him during the war. But it was customary for an officer to be addressed by the highest rank he had attained, so everyone called him General Custer.

And so it was General Custer who would be getting back into action again. But this time instead of fighting wild Rebels, he would be fighting wild Indians!

If Libbie thought that life with Custer would be exciting, she realized now that she was not to be disappointed.

# 12
# "Do Not Let Even a Dog Get Away!"

At about the same time that Custer was preparing to come to the plains, Red Cloud was preparing to fight the soldiers at Fort Kearny. In late fall of 1866, he felt he finally had enough warriors to do the job, and he and Crazy Horse started to make plans for the battle.

In December they decided the time was right to put their plans into action. They would use the classic Indian tactic — ambush! The Indians would pretend to attack the wood train, and when the soldiers came out to pursue them, they would be led into the ambush.

The Indians now only needed the decoy — the warriors who would lead the soldiers into the trap. "I and the other Shirt Wearers will be the decoys," said Crazy Horse.

Red Cloud agreed. If anyone could follow this plan, it would be Crazy Horse. So the attack was planned for the first good day following the full moon. Crazy Horse nodded. He would be ready. . . .

The day for the attack — December 21, by the white man's calendar — dawned sharp and cold. It was so cold that Crazy Horse did not strip for battle as he usually did. Today he wore a blanket belted around his slim, hard body. But he felt his medicine was good and everything would go well.

Even as he and his companions sat waiting on their war ponies, two thousand warriors were taking their places on either side of a place called Peno Valley. It was here that the Indians hoped to lure the soldiers when they came out of the fort.

The wait wasn't long.

As expected, they saw the wood train come out of the fort and head for the stand of trees. Crazy Horse watched with slitted eyes as the woodcutters made their way along the frozen ground. With him and the other Shirt Wearers were two Arapahoes and two Cheyenne. They were all hidden in a small gully so that they could not be seen from the fort.

As the wood train approached the stand of trees, the signal was given and a group of warriors swooped down and attacked. Soon the sharp crack of rifle fire, the yells of men, and the twang of bows shattered the peaceful silence of the wilderness.

As the battle continued, the gates of the fort swung open and a large relief column of troopers streamed out of the fort to the wood party's rescue.

Crazy Horse watched with satisfaction. *Hou!* It was good. The plan was working.

In command of the column was Captain William Fetterman. Like Lieutenant Grattan, who was killed in Conquering Bear's village, he was a headstrong officer just itching for a fight. He often bragged, "With eighty men, I can ride through the entire Sioux nation."

It was a strange quirk of fate that that happened to be the exact number of men he had under his command that day.

As Fetterman rode out of the fort, Crazy Horse yipped and spurred his pony out of hiding, followed by the rest of the decoy party. They wanted to be sure the soldiers saw them, so they yelled and howled and rode like demons.

And the soldiers saw them, all right. Fetterman wheeled his men around at the same time as a field artillery piece boomed out from the fort. The shot knocked one of the decoys from his horse and the rest of the party scattered in all directions, whooping and yelling as if they were terrified.

At that moment, Red Cloud, who had been overseeing the attack on the woodcutting party, called off his warriors. Fetterman believed he had the Indians on the run, since he saw that only the decoys were left, and they looked scared out of

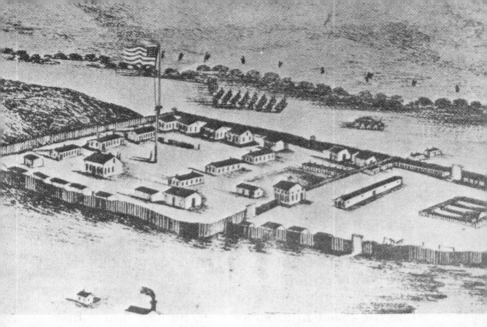

A drawing of Fort Phil Kearny

their wits. But he had to move forward slowly since about half of his command was infantry. To make sure he would keep the soldiers' attention, Crazy Horse whipped off his blanket and galloped toward Fetterman and his eighty men.

It looked to the soldiers as if he were trying to cover the retreat of the decoy party. When he got as close to the column as he dared, he reared up his pony and waved his blanket. There he stood like some wild spirit of the plains — his hair flowing free, his pony wheeling around and pawing the air, and his blanket snapping in the wind.

And as Crazy Horse waved his blanket, it was like waving a red flag before a bull. Fetterman yelled out a command and the soldiers moved forward and gave chase, all the while popping off shots in his direction.

Crazy Horse felt the blood rush to his head. He didn't even feel the cold, he was so filled with the heat of excitement. The soldiers drew closer and he wheeled his pony around and followed the rest of his party.

His heart pounded to the beat of his pony's hooves as he looked around and saw that the soldiers were still coming after him. The plan was working!

But he still must let the soldiers think they could catch him and the rest of the warriors in the party. So he used an old Indian trick. He stopped his pony for a moment and then, while pretending to beat his horse into a gallop with one hand, he actually reined it *back* with the other!

This gave the appearance that he was having trouble with his horse. The rest of the decoys stopped, too, as if they wanted to go to his aid.

Fetterman and his men yelled gleefully. Now they would teach these savages a lesson! As the column came closer, Crazy Horse again rode away. He made sure he was close enough to be tempting, but not close enough to be in range of the soldiers' guns. He followed just ahead of the soldiers and just a little behind his own men. The whole decoy party kept up the same pace. They knew if they pulled too far ahead of the troopers, the soldiers might give up and go back to the fort.

At one point, when the distance between the

decoy party and the troopers became too great, Crazy Horse once again used trickery. He leapt off his horse and sat down behind a bush. He was making believe that he and his pony were too tired to go on. The rest of the warriors circled around the area as if trying to protect him. Fetterman urged his men to go faster. Now he had them!

When the troopers came within firing range, the other Indians left, as if they were deserting Crazy Horse to the soldiers. Crazy Horse could see puffs of smoke coming from the soldiers' rifles and then the bullets came zinging near. All around him chunks of dirt and snow kicked up as the bullets plowed into the ground.

Then, just when it seemed that he must be caught, he leapt onto his pony and whipped it into a fast gallop after the rest of his party. On he went until he reached the ridge that sloped into Peno Valley on the other side. He stopped a moment and glanced over his shoulder. The soldiers were still coming!

Fetterman reached the ridge and kept coming down into the valley. "Come on!" he shouted. "We've got them now!" He couldn't know that warriors were hidden on each side of him, waiting until he and his whole command were completely in the valley.

When the last of the troopers shot into the valley, the signal was given and two thousand Sioux, Cheyenne, and Arapahoes came swarming down upon Fetterman and his men. Quickly cutting off his retreat, they struck at his flanks and front and rear. He was completely trapped!

The troopers tried to make a fight of it but their guns were no match for the hundreds and hundreds of arrows that hummed through the air like deadly hail. They clanged off canteens and rifles, skipped off rocks, and thudded into flesh and leather. The battlefield was so crowded with men that quite a few arrows missed their marks and hit other Indians.

It was like a weird, ghastly dance — the horses rearing and bucking and pawing the air, the troopers swiveling this way and that in their saddles, firing wildly, the infantrymen running around to take up defensive positions, the Indians circling, riding, shooting off their arrows with fluid, graceful motions.

The yells of the troopers, the screams of the Indians, the high-pitched neighing of the fear-crazed horses, and the crack of gunfire echoed down through the valley, a fit accompaniment to this dance of death.

In a shockingly short time it was all over. Every one of the eighty men in Fetterman's command was dead, including the captain himself. A deep silence came over the field of battle. The Indians could not at first realize that they had indeed killed every one of the hated soldiers. But there they were, spread out lifeless on the ground. Arrows bristled from every body, and the eyes that had only moments before took aim along rifles, were now closed in death.

Then, suddenly a frantic barking broke through the silence and a lone trooper's dog came loping out of some nearby rocks.

"Ahh, it is good that the dog is alive," said a Cheyenne. "Let it take the news of the soldiers' defeat back to the fort."

But another warrior slid an arrow onto his bow.

"No, do not let even a dog get away," he hissed.

The appearance of the dog broke the spell that had settled over the battlefield, and now the warriors screamed and yipped and slapped each other on the back. They had won a great victory!

## 13
## *The Burning Forts*

The victory the Indians had won at Fort Kearny swelled their confidence. In the summer of 1867, they decided to make a big effort against the white man, who had embedded himself in their land like a chigger, that pesky insect that buries its head under the skin and can only be removed by digging it out.

The fort was under a state of siege at this point. The soldiers had to fight their way through a ring of howling warriors every time they went for wood and water.

So a small force of troopers, under the command of Captain J. N. Powell, set up a miniature fort not far from Fort Kearny, on a small prairie near the pine woods. Now the woodcutters could be protected as soon as a hostile Indian showed his face.

The fort was made up of big wagon boxes that were formed into a circle. Inside the circle were tents for the men and an area for horses and mules.

Although it seemed as if this small "Box Fort" was little protection against the thousand or so fighting-mad Indians roaming the area, the soldiers had a great advantage. They had plenty of ammunition and were carrying the new breech-loading Springfield rifles. These rifles could be loaded and fired much faster than the old ones.

In contrast, the Indians had only about two hundred old rifles and very little ammunition. But Crazy Horse and Red Cloud decided to try the decoy trick again. They would attack a small woodcutters' camp less than a mile away from the Box Fort. When the soldiers came out of the Box Fort to rescue the woodcutters, Red Cloud would send the bulk of his warriors to attack *them*.

Once again, Crazy Horse would be in the decoy party. Like Custer, Crazy Horse loved to play tricks. But tricks that fooled the enemy, not tricks that made people laugh.

So just after dawn on the day of the attack, Crazy Horse, with his friend, Hump, his brother, Little Hawk, and a warrior named Little Big Man, rode off with two others to attack the woodcutters' camp and trick the enemy into an ambush. As the decoys rode off, a thousand armed warriors waited hidden in the hills behind them.

The decoy party was on its way to the camp when suddenly a sentry, who was patrolling the area between the Box Fort and the woodcutters' camp, spotted the decoys. The sharp crack of his rifle stung the air and a bullet whizzed dangerously close to Crazy Horse.

As if that had been a signal, the hidden warriors came swarming down from the hills, whooping and yelling and twanging their bows. Yells came from the Box Fort and puffs of white smoke and red flashes started to appear along the boxes as the soldiers began firing back. The little fort was on the alert now and all hopes for an ambush were gone.

Little Big Man

On top of that, the warriors fought in the old way — each one trying to show how brave he was, each one trying to outdo the others. There was no order, no leader, no commands.

Crazy Horse was angry at the warriors for spoiling the ambush and for showing such little discipline, but there was nothing to do now but join in the attack.

He and Hump gathered a large number of young men and started circling the fort. The ponies were fat and strong from eating the summer grass, and they carried the warriors swiftly along in a graceful, rhythmic motion.

Even as they defended themselves, the soldiers marveled at the Indians' horsemanship — riding flat against the flanks of their ponies while they yelled and whooped and shot arrows from underneath their horses' necks. It would have been a good show to watch if death weren't waiting in the wings.

Crazy Horse watched this wild ride around the fort with growing unease. He had thought that the soldiers' fire would slow down when they had to reload. But to his vast surprise, the shooting from the fort never slackened.

After five or six ponies went down riddled with bullets, Crazy Horse called off the circling. "Get to that ravine!" he yelled as he swung an arm in the direction of a nearby valley.

When the warriors assembled in the ravine, Crazy Horse said, "We must attack on foot."

The warriors nodded and, leaving their ponies out of range, they got ready for a foot charge. Some made their medicine to keep them safe over the open ground of the little prairie. Others tested the spring of their bows and grabbed handfuls of arrows.

Just as the soldiers were wondering what the Indians were up to, the warriors popped out of the ravine and the troopers saw a wave of whooping savages rushing toward them.

On they came through the green prairie grass — brown bodies painted red, white, yellow — black hair adorned with hawk and eagle feathers. Yipping, yowling, growling like bears, they zinged their arrows through the air with a *"Hoppo!"* — the call for charging the enemy. So many arrows hit the boxes that they were beginning to look like gigantic pin-cushions. To the white soldiers, the Indians seemed like painted madmen.

There were only forty men in the Box Fort and there were hundreds and hundreds of Indians attacking them. But they were all attacking in the same spot. It was easy for the soldiers to pick them off with their new fast-firing rifles. The troopers hardly took time to aim. They just poured bullet after bullet into the running, weaving, crouching wall of warriors before them.

Crazy Horse now realized that the soldiers had new weapons that could shoot faster than the old ones. Arrows and spears were no match for fast-flying bullets. "We are being butchered like the spotted buffalo!" he cried out.

"Ahhh!" A warrior with blood streaming down his yellow-painted shoulder agreed. "There seems no end to their shooting."

Just then, a scout galloped up on a foaming pony and yelled, "Many soldiers coming from the big fort, fast!"

That made Crazy Horse's mind up. He called off the attack and the warriors returned to their ponies and headed back into the hills.

This fight taught Crazy Horse a lesson. He now realized more than ever that to fight the whites, the Indians had to fight as one force and not individually as they were used to. But he also realized that even with that, they were no match for a fort that was defended with the new rifles the soldiers had.

The only way the Indian had a chance to win a fight with the white soldier now was out in the open on the plains. There, the speed, courage, and daring of the individual brave would equal the odds. He made up his mind never again to try to attack a force that held such a strong defensive position. He also made up his mind to try to teach his people the need for discipline and organized behavior in warfare against the whites.

But if Crazy Horse had a strong desire to fight the whites and push them back from the plains, not all Indians agreed with it. In fact, there were many who did not. These were the ones who wanted the good things the white man had — coffee, sugar, guns, ammunition, and cloth. Cloth was especially prized by the squaws, since it was much easier to work than buckskin and was much cooler to wear in the summer.

These Indians wanted to make peace with the whites so that they could have these things. But to earn these presents and others that the white man offered, one had to go to live on a reservation.

Reservations were areas of land that the government had put aside especially for the Indian to live on. The reservations were usually quite large, but the Indians had to stay on them and were not free to roam the whole land as they had been used to. For Red Cloud, Crazy Horse, and the rest of the hostile warriors, that would be like being in prison.

All the same, General Sherman, who was in charge of the Indian territory, offered to talk peace with Red Cloud. But Red Cloud and Crazy Horse said that there could be no peace until the soldiers left the forts in the Powder River Country. Sherman was not willing to do this, so the peace proposal died almost before it was born. But Sherman did not have enough men or equipment to wage a large war against the Sioux at the moment, so a sort of truce came over the plains.

Crazy Horse spent the winter of that year living the free life he loved. He hunted so that the poor and helpless people in his tribe could be fed and sheltered. For this was what he did for a living, so to speak — he was a hunter. Being a warrior was only part of his duties to his society. To be sure, he was a warrior more often than not, but that was only because there always seemed to be someone to fight. But the people appreciated his help and generosity as a hunter as much as they respected him as a warrior.

That same winter of 1867-68, Custer and Libbie were at a place called Fort Leavenworth, in Kansas. After only about a year in action on the plains, Custer found himself suspended from duty.

He had been found guilty, among other things, of calling off a campaign against the Indians without authority and shooting some deserters without a trial.

Custer had fought the charges, but lost the case in the end. But with his usual devil-may-care attitude, the punishment didn't bother him, and he and Libbie proceeded to enjoy his temporary retirement at the fort.

Fort Leavenworth was the largest post on the frontier and there were enough parties, dances, parades, and good hunting to satisfy them both. Custer was also living the life he loved.

Meanwhile, the war up north had now settled into a stalemate. Crazy Horse and Red Cloud were unwilling to try to attack the main fort head on and the whites were unwilling to use the Bozeman Trail. So the forts along the Bozeman Trail became little islands surrounded by a sea of plains. And the Indians lived well on this prairie ocean, eating buffalo meat and wild fruits while the soldiers forced down stale bread and beans.

Once again General Sherman proposed peace. It wasn't just that he was giving in to the Indians' demands. He needed soldiers to fight the hostile Cheyennes, southern Oglala, Arapahoes, and other tribes on the warpath on the Central Plains, and the soldiers at the forts would supply that need. But once again Red Cloud said that there would be no peace until the soldiers had actually left the forts.

Finally Sherman agreed to his terms, and within days all the troops at the forts along the Bozeman Trail marched out and left them deserted. Then the Indians under Crazy Horse swarmed down on the forts. For days, the crackle of flames mingled with the victory whoops of the warriors as Crazy Horse and his band burned every last one to the ground. Only then did Red Cloud and the other chiefs come and touch the pen to the new treaty.

Crazy Horse stayed away, however. He was unwilling to come to any white man's council. But he was happy about how things had turned out. He felt that he had played a big role in turning back the white invaders from his land. For the first time in his life, he would be free of whites!

*Ho-ka hey!* It was a good time to live!

# 14
## Custer the Indian Fighter

**E**ven as the Indian war with Red Cloud in the north was cooling down, the Indian war south of the Powder River Country in Kansas was heating up.

The southern Oglala Sioux, the Cheyennes, the Arapahoes, and other tribes were on the warpath. Again it was a matter of protecting their living space. The railroads were pushing ever westward, and the white buffalo hunters were killing off the herd in Kansas at an alarming rate. The hostiles had heard of the Red Cloud victory in the north and they had high hopes they could achieve a similar victory themselves.

So it was that in November 1868, just a week after the treaty with Red Cloud had been signed, Custer found himself back in command of the

Custer with his
wife, Libbie,
and his brother Tom

Seventh Cavalry and scouring the southern plains for hostile Indians.

Custer had, of course, heard of the Fetterman disaster so he had no illusions about how Indians fought. He no longer thought of them as noble red men, as he had done at West Point, but as uncivilized primitives. Yet he had to admit that they had a savage dignity, and he had to admire the daring and courage of their warriors. The name Crazy Horse had come to his attention — although the newspapers didn't know of him yet — through the army grapevine. The story of the Fetterman massacre was still widely talked about in army camps.

With Custer was his brother Tom, who had also

joined the army, following in Armstrong's footsteps, and was now an officer. Custer liked to surround himself with family and friends, and even various pets—especially dogs. Perhaps he remembered how his hero Ned Hazard in *Swallow Barn* always had a pack of hounds following him. He still loved music, so he was sure that he had a military band along with him out on the plains. This way he could have music to listen to, to march to, and even to fight to!

The little boy in him still loved practical jokes and horseplay, and even in the midst of danger, he and his brother could find something funny to do, or someone to play a joke on.

In November of 1868, Custer was given orders to find and destory the hostile Indians who were making raids into Kansas and Texas and attacking and killing white settlers with alarming aggression.

He was to start out from a place called Camp Supply with eight hundred men and a number of Osage Indian scouts. The army frequently employed friendly Indians as scouts since they were far better at following tracks than the average white soldier.

On the day the expedition was to leave, it had started to snow, but instead of letting the weather stop him, Custer said, "This is just what we want." It would be easy to track Indians in the snow because the marks of their passage would be plain to see.

So with high spirits he told his band, who were all mounted on beautiful gray horses, to play "The Girl I Left Behind Me." With the music blaring in the thin cold air, and the soldiers who had stayed behind wishing them good luck, the column marched away into the swirling snowstorm.

Out in the snowy wilderness a few days later, a scout reported signs that an Indian village was camped by the Washita, a small stream not too far off from where Custer and his men were. Leaving eighty men to guard the wagon train that contained all their supplies, he told his officers that the troopers must take one hundred rounds of ammunition, some coffee and hard bread, but no extra blankets. He didn't want any extra weight to slow down the men. Then he looked at his watch and said, "In twenty minutes, gentlemen, the advance will be sounded."

The officers wheeled their horses and galloped to their commands. Ammunition was given out to each man along with a ration of hard bread. Some of the soldiers put on a double pair of red flannel underwear, too. Without extra blankets, it was going to be hard to keep out the bitter cold.

It was nighttime when the command moved out and the column made its way silently in the dim light of the moon. The soldiers spoke in whispers and kept the tin cups that dangled under their saddlebags from rattling. A while later, Custer saw one of the Osage Indians, who had been riding ahead of the column, dismount and crouch down on a ridge up ahead. He dismounted also and crept up alongside the scout. The man silently pointed downward.

"Heap Injuns down there," he whispered.

Custer peered into the darkness and saw a herd of animals. Were they Indian ponies or buffalo? It was hard to tell from where they were. If they were buffalo, it meant nothing. But if they were ponies, it meant that a war party or the village would be right ahead. Suddenly a dog barked and moments later a baby cried. Warriors do not take dogs or babies on war parties. It had to be the Indian village!

Custer made his way back to his men and sent for his officers. It was now past midnight. When the officers came up, they huddled around their leader like a sports team listening to its captain.

"We will divide the regiment into four detachments," he whispered in his fast, excited way, almost stuttering. "Each detachment will attack the village from four different directions at my signal."

The officers nodded eagerly. But the Indian scouts were less than eager. They didn't like attacking a village where the number of warriors was unknown. What if they were outnumbered?

But it was Custer's way, as it had been in the

Civil War, to attack first. If outnumbered, Custer would cut his way back.

"Take your detachments and surround the village from three sides, and be sure to do it silently," he ordered.

"I will stay here with the fourth detachment," he continued, "and we will attack at dawn."

The officers nodded again and went back to their commands.

Custer wrapped the cape of his heavy coat around his head and went to lie down on a buffalo robe in the snow. As always, he hated to wait for anything. Action was what he wanted, and the sooner the better.

But the warmth of the buffalo robe and the tang of the cold air in his lungs soon lulled him into a fitful sleep. . . .

When dawn broke crisp and cold, Custer was wide awake. In the dim light he could now see the tops of the tepees through the tangled black branches of bare trees. He ordered his men to mount and form a line, even the members of the military band. When everyone was ready, he raised his arm. Suddenly a shot rang out from somewhere in the village. At that, Custer turned to the band leader and told him to play "Garry Owen." That was a fast, rowdy tune that he and his men especially liked.

As the jaunty air blared across the snow, Custer heard cheers from the soldiers in place on the other sides of the village. The soldiers charged from all sides, yelling, and their guns booming.

The Indians, taken completely by surprise, tumbled out of the warmth of their tepees into the fearful cold of the snow-covered landscape.

The strange music blaring through the air, the boom of the guns, the yells of the troopers, all terrified them in their sleepy confusion. And the sight of the soldiers rushing at them from out of the darkness, the horses' hooves thudding on the snow-packed earth, making a noise like rolling thunder, routed them completely.

But even so, those that could fought back valiantly. Some of the braves were totally naked and ran out of their lodges with just their weapons in their hands. Some jumped into the waist-deep freezing-cold Washita and returned the fire from the protection of its banks. But it was all in vain. The troopers cut through the village like a pack of wild demons — shooting at anything that crossed their path. It was hard to see in the dim light who they were shooting at — squaws, braves, or even children.

By ten o'clock that morning, a few scattered warriors fought on, but the battle was as good as over. At least a hundred Indians lay dead on the ground. A few had escaped, but Custer had taken fifty-three women and children prisoner.

Custer rode around the battlefield to see the wounded and dead. At one point he saw a bugler — no more than a boy — with two wounds in his head. The lad was alive and sitting on a bunch of buffalo robes. He told Custer that he had been hit by an arrow that had entered over his eye and come out by his ear! But the shaft had not penetrated his skull, it had merely glanced around it. A surgeon had removed the shaft and the boy was none the worse for wear except for the burning wound underneath his skin.

Custer asked if the boy had seen his attacker.

"If anybody thinks I didn't see him," the boy answered, holding up a fresh scalp, "I want them to take a look at that."

It seemed that even a boy could be caught up in the violence of battle.

After the Battle of the Washita, as this fight came to be called, Custer and the Seventh Cavalry were commended for an outstanding victory against the hostiles.

There were some, however, who said that the village had not been hostile at all, and that the head of the village, a chief called Black Kettle, had been friendly to the whites. But Custer and his men had found photographs, bits of bedding, and letters belonging to Kansas settlers. To him, that was proof enough that at least some, if not all, of the warriors in the camp had been involved with raids into Kansas.

With this battle, the fame of Custer and the Seventh Cavalry as Indian fighters began to spread.

They had a number of other battles after this, and in one, Custer and his men rescued two captive white women who were being held for ransom by the Cheyenne.

General Sherman was impressed with their performance in the field. The hostiles were now under control and Custer and the Seventh Cavalry had been foremost in bringing that about. It looked as if the war on the southern plains had calmed down, at least for the time being.

# 15
# *War to the Bitter End!*

**I**f the hostiles on the southern plains were defeated, Crazy Horse and the rest of the warriors up in the Powder River country were not.

While Custer had been roaming the southern plains winning battles, Crazy Horse and the other hostiles had been living free — hunting, socializing, and making war on the Shoshonis and the Crows. The hated forts were gone, and with them the soldiers. There was nothing to stop them now from living the life they chose.

They had piled up an immense supply of buffalo robes, and they wanted to go and trade with the white man down by the North Platte River around Fort Laramie.

Many of these Indians, including Crazy Horse, had grown used to the white man's goods, like coffee and sugar, blankets and utensils, and guns and ammunition.

But when the great camp arrived to trade, the soldiers turned them back by force. General Sherman felt that if the Indians wanted the white man's goods, they should come and stay on the reservations. If they wanted to live the wild, free life, they should take care of themselves.

He also wanted to keep firearms from the Indians, who claimed they wanted them only for hunting. But as everyone knew, guns could be used as easily for war. Sherman knew that sooner or later a big battle would be fought to decide once and for all who governed the land: the Indians or the United States of America and the less guns in Indian hands, the better.

The government felt it had a just claim. Immigrants were pouring into the United States from Europe, and land was needed to feed and settle the growing population. And aside from this, the United States was determined to stretch its boundaries across the whole continent. If the Indians had been allowed to live the way they wanted to, they would take up an enormous amount of land just to support their way of life. And that was based on roaming far and wide, hunting for buffalo and other game, and generally moving about whenever and wherever they wanted. In this respect, they felt — especially the hostiles — that the whole plains were their domain.

The United States, on the other hand, was trying to be as fair as possible within the limits of its policy of expansion. The government did not *want* to fight the Indians. What it did want was for the Indians to finally accept the ways of civilization and become part of the citizenry. The hostiles, of course, disagreed with this completely.

They considered the land to be theirs in the first place, and who were the whites to tell them how or where they should live on it? And as for becoming "civilized," they were perfectly happy with their life as it was and saw no need to change it to suit the white man.

General Sherman's policy of keeping the Indians from trading soon led to a split in the Sioux camp. Red Cloud was beginning to think that it was better to live on the reservation than to struggle against the soldiers and the elements at the same time. Each year fewer and fewer buffalo roamed the plains and without the buffalo, the red man's way of life was endangered.

So he and more than half the hostiles finally came in and settled at an agency south of the Black Hills named, aptly enough, Red Cloud Agency. The agency was a small group of buildings where the Government Indian Agent and the Army had their headquarters. The area for miles around was where the Indians set up their tepees and, in effect, their reservation.

Crazy Horse and the other hostiles, however,

stayed in the Powder River country, determined to resist the whites at all costs.

For a short time things went smoothly at the Agency. But soon after that, Red Cloud had so many complaints about his tribe's treatment, that the whites took him to Washington to meet the President and tell him personally. During the course of that trip, he was also taken to Omaha, Chicago, and even New York. He was so impressed by what he saw and the white man's power, that he realized more than ever that the Indian could never win a war against so powerful an enemy.

When he finally got back to the plains, this great chief put away his warrior's clothing, and from then on, was concerned only with trying to better the lot of his people through peaceful means. The Indians who didn't agree with his policy drifted back to the Powder River country to join Crazy Horse.

With Red Cloud now out of the fight, Crazy Horse became the foremost warrior of his people. And he adamantly preached war against the whites.

But his attitude did not stop him and his people from trading with the whites whenever they could. In spite of the ban against trading with the hostiles, some white traders did manage to sneak into the Indian camps with a number of goods.

One of these traders brought newspapers with him from that strange and far-distant place the white man called civilization. He read accounts to Crazy Horse describing Indians as blood-thirsty savages. One of the newspapers happened to have a picture in it drawn by some eastern artist who had probably never been west of the Mississippi. It showed a group of naked, whooping Indians dangling bloody scalps in their hands and dancing around three little white girls whom they had captured and tied to the door of a burning house.

Crazy Horse grew hot with anger at the picture. That was not the way the Indian was, he said. Children were not mistreated in that manner. Warriors prided themselves in fighting an enemy who fought back, not in killing and frightening defenseless children!

To Crazy Horse it was one more example of the lies and treachery of the whites. One more example of why the tracks of moccasins and boots could not run together on the land.

But with Red Cloud and a large number of hostiles on the reservation, a peace of sorts settled over the Powder River country.

In 1871 Crazy Horse and his people started to drift northward toward the Yellowstone River in Montana. Crazy Horse wanted to get as far away from the whites as he could. He and his people camped near the Yellowstone together with the wild Sioux of the north country. There, Crazy Horse and his people mingled with the Miniconjous, Sans Arcs, and the Hunkpapa Sioux of the great chief Sitting Bull.

Sitting Bull

Crazy Horse and Sitting Bull became good friends. They were drawn together because of their mutual desire to resist the whites at any cost. Like Red Cloud had been, Sitting Bull was now the overall leader in the Indians' fight to rid themselves of the white scourge. And once again, Crazy Horse was the warrior who could put his plans into action.

Sitting Bull was known as a good medicine man. On top of that, he knew how to lead his people. He told the Sioux many times that he was not made to be a reservation Indian. The Great Spirit had made him a free Indian to go where he wanted to go, to hunt buffalo, and to be a big leader in his tribe.

For a time it seemed as if the Sioux could live the life they loved without being bothered by the whites. But the whites had other plans.

In 1872, the Northern Pacific railroad was pushing westward up to the Missouri River. This was only about two hundred miles or so from the Yellowstone country where Crazy Horse and his people were. Once again the whites were pressing against the Indians.

On one expedition, surveyors for the railroad were moving along the valley of the Yellowstone to map out the possible route of the new line. They had a strong military escort with them. When Indian scouts reported this, the Indians went out to meet the troopers. There was a long drawn-out fight. Neither side won, but the troopers and the survey party retreated nonetheless.

To the Indians, this was a great victory. They had shown the soldiers that they were there in force and willing to fight. They didn't know, however, that the white surveyors had gone as far as they had wanted to at the time and therefore saw no reason to fight their way farther.

After this fight, Crazy Horse and Sitting Bull went back to their people and took up where they had left off. Crazy Horse even found time to get married. His wife's name was Black Shawl and she was the sister of a friend of his, a warrior named Red Feather.

As was the custom among the Sioux, his mother-in-law came to live in their tepee and with two women to take care of him, Crazy Horse had a comfortable home life indeed.

Within a year, Black Shawl gave birth. The day it happened, she brought the baby, wrapped in a doeskin bundle, into the tepee. Crazy Horse had been dozing and looked at her with the sleep still in his eyes.

Black Shawl put the tiny bundle down and looked at Crazy Horse. "It is a girl," she said sadly — for she knew as everyone else in the tribe did that every Indian man wishes a warrior son. But Crazy Horse gently lifted the tiny bundle and smiled.

"*Hou!*" he said. "Then it is a new daughter for the Oglalas. She will grow up to be a great mother for the people. Everyone will stand in wonder of her holy ways and will be quiet. I shall call her, They-Are-Afraid-of-Her!"

Crazy Horse was delighted with his new daughter and spent many happy hours playing with her. He also spent a lot of time now with the young people of the tribe. Crazy Horse became a storyteller — telling them about the old ways and how they were good. He schooled the boys in the arts of living free on the plains. He taught them how to make a bow and arrow, how to hunt, and how to fight.

*Hou!* Life was good!

# 16
## The Paths of the
## Two Warriors Cross

If life seemed good to Crazy Horse, it seemed boring to Custer. He was now living in Kentucky with Libbie in a small brick cottage. Although he was kept busy with army business, he missed the free life of the plains and longed to be back there. Like Crazy Horse, he couldn't stand being cooped up. And anywhere but the wide-open plains meant being cooped up to Custer.

But in February of 1873, he finally got orders that sent his spirits soaring. He was to gather together the Seventh Cavalry once more and proceed to Fort Abraham Lincoln, which was in Dakota territory and near the Yellowstone country. The Northern Pacific railroad was finally about to enter Indian territory, territory that the Sioux claimed was theirs because of the treaty that Red

Cloud had signed. General Sherman knew there was going to be big trouble, and he wanted Custer on the job to protect the advancing railroad.

Custer was as happy as a kid when he heard the news. He yelled "Hee-haa!" and waltzed around the living room of their cottage, humming a snappy tune. He laughed and talked so fast that Libbie could hardly understand what he was saying. Custer picked her up in his strong arms and put her on top of a table so that he could throw furniture around the room like a wild kid. He was crazy with joy. At last he was going back to what his whole body and soul thirsted for — action, adventure, and fighting!

If he and Crazy Horse had anything in common, it was this. They were both born to be warriors. It was true that each fought for what he believed in, but it was also true that each just loved to fight — anytime, anyplace. Having a cause to fight for was just a happy coincidence.

So in the spring of 1873, Custer started back toward the land and life he loved. The Northern Pacific railroad had not yet reached the Yellowstone River country, where the Sioux hostiles were, but it was headed there. Custer's job was to drive the Sioux out of the way.

The time had now come when the two warriors were galloping along the same path, headed toward one another. It was only a matter of time before they must meet.

That summer, Custer and the Seventh Cavalry

were a fine sight: lean, hard soldiers with sun-burned faces. Their large horses trotted easily along; their swallow-tailed flags snapped sharply in the breeze. The buglers, the band, the fighting men, and ahead of them all, the boy general with the flowing locks, George Armstrong Custer!

With Custer was his brother Tom and a group of officers who were friends from the Civil War. As usual, he also had a gang of pets along. Cages of mockingbirds and canaries, and even a litter of puppies rode in the wagons. That was the way Custer always liked to travel — even into hostile territory — surrounded by family, friends, and pets. And of course, any time he could he also added his pretty wife, Libbie, to the list.

Fort Lincoln was right on the fringe of hostile territory — only 200 miles from the heart of the Sioux country. It was one of a number of forts that encircled the Sioux in readiness for the showdown which everyone knew was coming.

The surveyors for the railroad were edging ever closer to the Sioux. The railroad was planned to run along the north bank of the Yellowstone River. The hostiles claimed that this was their territory and that it extended all the way up to the Canadian border, one hundred and fifty miles away.

It was plain to see that no one was going to give in. The government wanted the railroad built; the Sioux wanted it stopped. The stage was set for a final showdown, and Custer and Crazy Horse were in the wings. But neither one was waiting for their cue.

One hot summer day Custer and the Seventh Cavalry were on an expedition inside Sioux territory. The expedition was made up of cavalry, infantry, and surveyors. Wagon trains full of supplies followed. The cavalry was in the lead, keeping a sharp eye out for hostiles. And the hostiles were well aware of the expedition. They could hardly miss discovering the lumbering parade as it made its way through the empty landscape.

The expedition weaved through grassy meadows, groves of cottonwood trees, and endless flat plains on its way into the wilderness.

Custer by his tent on the expedition guarding the construction of the Northern Pacific Railroad

At noon, as white, flat-bottomed clouds with billowy tops sailed across the blue sky, Custer halted the cavalry near the mouth of the Tongue River to allow the rest of the expedition to catch up. It was a hot, dusty day, and the men pulled the saddles off their horses and rested beneath the welcome shade of cottonwood trees. Custer, too, took his saddle to use as a headrest, and walked over to a large tree. He had taken off his buckskin shirt and boots, and soon he was lying down and dozing comfortably under the shade of rustling leaves.

In the meantime, Crazy Horse and Sitting Bull, looking for a good place to set up an ambush, had been tracking Custer closely. Now, while the column was halted, Crazy Horse and his warriors climbed to the top of a nearby bluff to spy on their position. With eyes narrowed against the sunlight, Crazy Horse peered down on the troopers.

Good, they were resting. That meant that they hadn't detected the Indian presence. Then his eyes went to the lone sleeping man under the cottonwood tree. He had heard of Custer, the one they called *Tongo Nasu*, the "Long-hair," and realized that this must be him. He looked at Custer with interest. So this is how the famous Indian fighter conducts himself in enemy territory in the middle of the day — by taking a nap! Crazy Horse smiled. He would soon wake the white chief up from his dreams!

The plan for the attack was simple. A decoy party would lure the soldiers into a nearby stand of timber where the rest of the war party would lie hidden.

Crazy Horse crept down from his lookout perch and made ready to put the plan into action. He gathered the decoy party together and when the warriors were in place in the timber, gave the signal to start. With a whoop, the decoys kicked their ponies into a fast gallop. . . .

"Indians! Indians!" the sentries cried, as they saw Crazy Horse and the other warriors charging into the troopers' herd of horses.

The alarm roused the dozing troopers into full awareness. Some ran for their horses, while others struggled back into their boots. Custer snatched his Remington rifle and ran for his horse, still in his socks and undershirt. But the decoys had now retreated to a safe distance and started to whoop and yell and taunt him with insults. Custer pulled on his boots and shirt and ordered the men to mount. Taking a detail of twenty men, he raced after the decoys, who were heading for a stand of timber. But as he approached the woods, he became suspicious.

"Careful," he shouted in his high-pitched voice. "It might be an ambush!" But still he came on.

Good, thought Crazy Horse, the ambush was working!

But suddenly a group of Cheyenne who were in the war party recognized Custer as the hated Long-hair who had attacked their village on the

Washita and killed their relatives. The Cheyenne were so bent on revenge that they sprang from the timber before the trap had been closed. The other warriors had no choice but to follow them. The ambush was ruined.

When Custer saw the screaming, yipping braves riding out of the timber, he reared up his horse and ordered a retreat. The troopers spurred their big American horses back the way they had come. The Indians followed, but the long-legged cavalry horses were faster than Indian ponies, and Custer made it safely back.

When they got back to the regiment, the troopers dismounted and fought the warriors on foot. The Indian riders made easy targets for the steady fire of the soldiers.

Then at one point, Custer ordered the men to mount and form a line. With a whoop he ordered a charge and the troopers thundered toward the largest group of warriors. The Indians scattered like a herd of buffalo before the blue-clad line of troopers, and sped off into the distance.

With this the fight ended, and Custer called his officers together to review the action. Four of their company had been killed, but the troopers had made a good fight of it.

For the next few days Custer trailed the Indians looking for another chance to get at them. He got that opportunity a few days later, but after another fierce battle, each side withdrew. Crazy Horse, Sitting Bull, and the rest of the warriors then went back to the Powder River country.

Custer returned to Fort Lincoln, where he was joined by Libbie. They moved into a new house, which had been built for Custer as the commander of the fort, and set up housekeeping.

Libbie made sure the house was furnished as befitted the commander of the fort. Fancy kerosene lamps brought from the East hung from a high ceiling and heavy, lush drapes hung from the windows. The parlor was cozily furnished with overstuffed sofas, chairs, and a number of footstools for Custer to prop his feet on and relax at the end of the day.

He could relax a bit now. He felt that he had won a victory over the Indians and had taught them a good lesson. The Indians, on the other hand, felt exactly the same way about Custer and his men.

# 17
# *The Black Hills*

**F**or a while it looked to the Indians as though they had concrete proof of their victory because suddenly the railroad stopped sending surveyors into their territory. To the Indians, this looked as if they had won their fight.

The real reason the railroad company had stopped surveying, however, was that it had run out of money for the time being. All construction had come to a halt, and so once again, a shaky peace settled over the plains.

But in 1874, something happened that shattered this fragile peace. . . .

The Black Hills that lay between the Dakota and Wyoming Territories were sacred to the Indians.

## The Black Hills Expedition

These hills were granted to them forever by the treaty of 1868. The Indians called the hills *Pa Sapa*, and to them it was a holy place where the gods dwelled.

In 1874, ten troops of the Seventh Cavalry, two infantry companies, a photographer, a herd of cattle, three Gatling guns, a cannon, Custer's band, and over a hundred wagons marched into the wilderness and headed for the Black Hills.

The government said that the purpose of the expedition was scientific — to learn as much as possible about this relatively unexplored part of the country. But there was another purpose to the expedition, and that was to see if the rumors were true. Rumors saying that the most valuable of metals to the white man could be found there in vast quantities — gold!

The Indians were outraged by this trespassing on their sacred ground, and watched with smoldering anger as the wagon train weaved its way into the mountains.

But the expedition went its way unhindered and before long, the rumors had proven to be well-founded. There *was* gold to be had there. Custer himself reported that there was gold among the grass roots, and gold in every stream.

When the expedition returned, the news spread like a prairie fire. It was plain to see that this information would send prospectors rushing into the hills in search of the yellow metal.

And rush they did — in droves. The government was embarrassed. The Black Hills were indeed promised to the Indians by the treaty of 1868 and the government had no legal claims to it. But the gold prospectors kept coming, in spite of the dangers of finding arrows in their bodies instead of gold in their hands.

In 1875, in answer to its problem, the United States Government offered to buy the Black Hills. This offer immediately set up a sharp division in the Indian camp. Red Cloud was willing to talk about it. He knew by now that if the white man did not get what he wanted by peaceful means, he would find an excuse to fight for it. And he also knew that the whites had the power behind them to win. An Indian defeat in a war would leave the Indian with nothing but dust in his mouth. If the Indians could get a good price for the land, that at least would be better than nothing.

But Crazy Horse and Sitting Bull would not hear of it. To them, no Indian land was for sale no matter what the price, least of all the Black Hills.

The government, seeing that a stalemate had been reached, tried to force the issue. They sent out an order that all the wild tribes in Indian Territory had to go to the reservations or be considered hostile and the army would come after them. This seemed like a stern order, but it was really directed at Crazy Horse, Sitting Bull, and the rest of the hostiles. The government knew that the hostiles were the only ones who were standing in the way of the purchase of the Black Hills and of the advance of the Northern Pacific railroad. They had to be put on reservations or driven out of the way.

Of course, Crazy Horse and Sitting Bull ignored the order. They knew that this meant war, but they felt they had been pushed far enough. It was time to take a stand and make a fight of it. And Crazy Horse knew that this time, it would be a fight to the death between the white man and the red man for possession of the plains.

Even Custer wrote at the time, "If I were an

Indian, I would greatly prefer to cast my lot among those of my people who adhered to the free open plains rather than submit to the confined limits of a reservation. . . ."

Here again was the irony of the Indian problem. Many white soldiers did not hate the Indians and many even sympathized with them. But they had a job to do and if that job meant herding Indians onto reservations, whether they wanted to go or not, they had to do it. If some who resisted were killed in the process, that was unfortunate, but that was the way it was.

On the other hand, many Indians did not hate the white man, either, but they also had a job to do and that was to keep the whites from pushing them off lands they felt belonged to them.

But the whites should not be singled out as the first and only villains in this fight for land. The Indians themselves had competed with each other for land they had wanted.

The Sioux had been driven westward onto the plains by the Ojibwa, Chippewa, and other hostile eastern tribes. The Sioux in turn drove the Crows and other tribes off land they wanted. And so it went on, the more powerful tribes always taking what they wanted from the weaker. And the whites were no better or worse than their red-skinned brothers. In fact, it would be safe to say that if roles were reversed, it might have been the "civilized" Indians who would be driving the white "savages" off the land and putting them on reservations!

Be that as it may, in the spring of 1876, the army decided to send a large force into Sioux territory and deal with Sitting Bull and Crazy Horse once and for all.

# 18
# *The March to Death*

On May 17, 1876, a large force under the command of General Alfred Terry left Fort Lincoln on what was to be a major, and it was hoped, a final, military operation against the hostiles. The army was planning a three-pronged attack. General Alfred Terry and his command would start out from Fort Lincoln together with Custer at the head of the Seventh Cavalry.

A second force under the command of General George Crook would start out from Fort Fetterman and move toward the Little Bighorn River. A third column under the command of Major-General John Gibbon would follow the Yellowstone River downstream from Fort Ellis in Montana territory.

These three military expeditions — Terry's,

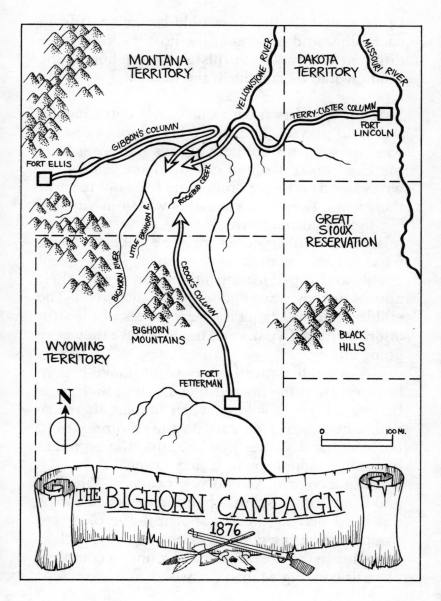

MONTANA
TERRITORY

DAKOTA
TERRITORY

YELLOWSTONE RIVER

MISSOURI RIVER

TERRY-CUSTER COLUMN

GIBBON'S COLUMN

FORT
LINCOLN

FORT ELLIS

ROSEBUD CREEK

LITTLE BIGHORN R.

BIGHORN RIVER

GREAT
SIOUX
RESERVATION

CROOK'S COLUMN

BIGHORN
MOUNTAINS

WYOMING
TERRITORY

BLACK
HILLS

FORT
FETTERMAN

N

0          100 MI.

THE BIGHORN CAMPAIGN
1876

Crook's, and Gibbon's — would be far apart from each other and coming at the hostiles from three different directions. In this way, they hoped, the Sioux would be caught in the middle.

As the expedition with Custer left Fort Lincoln, the band played "The Girl I Left Behind Me." It was the song the soldiers always played as they marched away from their loved ones. Officers' wives stood on their porches and tried not to show their tears. Everyone knew this was going to be a big fight, and many wives were afraid that their husbands would not return. The enlisted men's wives were more demonstrative. They wept openly and wiped tears from their eyes with their aprons as they waved good-bye to their men. The children, not realizing the seriousness of the situation, beat on tin pans and made believe they were going along.

Custer smiled at this show of make-believe bravery. He remembered that he, too, had made believe he was a soldier when he was their age and wore a velveteen suit. As the column moved out, the band swung into the tune the regiment had now made its own, "Garry Owen."

It was a colorful and noisy procession — the Ree and Crow Indian scouts chanting their war songs, the band playing, horses snorting, the blue-clad troopers shouting good-byes, the regimental flags snapping in the breeze, and the sound of countless utensils banging against tin, wood, and leather. At the head of it all rode Custer in a fringed buckskin shirt, red tie, and a white broad-brimmed hat.

Libbie at first was thrilled at the sight of it as she rode by Custer's side. She and a few others were going along for the first day's march. But her happy frame of mind soon changed to gloomy thoughts because a strange thing happened as the column moved out of the fort.

There was a mist in the air that morning and by some quirk of nature, and a trick of the light, a mirage appeared in the sky above them. Suddenly she could see the whole two-mile column of troopers, scouts, and white canvas-topped wagons mirrored above them, marching into the sky. To Libbie, it was a foretelling of disaster.

But to Custer, it was merely a mirage — no more and no less. He and his men were strong and confident, and he laughed and joked with his brother Tom as always. And this time there was more to be gay about than usual. He had more family members and friends along than ever before. Besides Tom, there was another younger brother named Boston — Bos for short. Then there was Autie Reed, a teenaged nephew who was named after him. Custer's brother-in-law, Lieutenant James Calhoun, was joining him, along with a gang of old friends and comrades-in-arms. Of course his ever-present pack of hunting dogs was there, too.

Everyone was so jolly it seemed as if they were all going on a picnic instead of a military expedition. Autie Reed was hoping to get some Indian souvenirs before the expedition was over, and looked forward to the coming conflict as no more than an exciting adventure.

Weeks went by as the Terry and Custer expedition wound its way farther and farther into the wilderness. Finally, as had been previously planned, they met up with Gibbon. General Crook, in the meantime, was supposed to be marching up from the south.

At this point, Terry sent Major Marcus Reno, one of Custer's officers, on a scouting mission to seek out any signs of the hostiles. When Reno returned, days later, he reported that he had found an Indian trail of over three hundred lodges going toward the Greasy Grass, the Indian name for the Little Bighorn.

An Indian trail on soft ground was easy to follow, since the Indians carried their goods on travois poles. These were long wooden poles that were tied to their ponies and dragged behind them on the ground. The Indians would load all their belongings in a net or on a platform between these poles and tie them in place. The poles made long tracks in the ground as the Indians traveled. It was then simple to guess about how many Indians had passed along a certain route by counting the pairs of furrows dug into the earth.

A large number of ponies meant a large number of Indians. One could also see how many tepees had been put up at a certain spot because the circles where they had stood could still be seen on the ground. Again, a large number of lodges or tepees meant a large number of Indians.

On June 22, after a conference between Terry, Custer, and Gibbon, it was decided that Custer should take the Seventh Cavalry and follow the trail that Reno had discovered. It was hoped he would then find the exact location of the hostile camp.

On June 24, the Seventh Cavalry was on the move following the Indian trail. Custer's orders were that if he found the Indians, he should take whatever action he saw fit. It was believed that the Indians were camped somewhere near the Little Bighorn River.

The main reason for the expedition, however, was not to kill or defeat the Indians, but to round them up and escort them to the reservations. And the most important thing was to keep the Indians from escaping and melting away into the countryside as they had done so many times before.

But in spite of this, Custer expected a fight and was, in fact, preparing for one.

As the column marched nearer and nearer to the valley of the Little Bighorn, they saw many signs that a large number of Indians had passed that way recently, all heading for the Little Bighorn. They found drawings in the sand left by the hostiles, predicting that all the soldiers who followed them would be killed. A fresh white man's scalp hung from a pole at another place. Custer laughed at these warnings. He had been warned by Indians before and had always come out a victor.

But there was one more warning that was less easy to laugh away, especially for his men and the Indian scouts, and that was the finding of a recently used site for a Sun Dance.

The Sun Dance was usually practiced by the Sioux and Cheyenne before going on the warpath. But they also practiced it each summer as a test of strength and endurance.

The warriors, or dancers, as they were called, would gather in a huge circle about two hundred feet in circumference with an opening pointing toward the east, where the sun is born each morning and where they would pray to the Great Spirit: *wakan tanka*. A huge pole about thirty feet high, cut from a sacred cottonwood tree and painted blue, green, yellow, and red to represent the four directions, would be placed in the center of the circle. From this pole dangled rawhide or buffalo-hair ropes, one for each dancer.

A medicine man would then cut gashes into the chests of the dancers and sticks would be shoved into the skin and underneath the muscles and then attached to the dangling rope ends. The ropes would be tightened so that the dancer was forced to stand on tiptoe, which would force the muscles three or four inches out of his body! There were even more painful ways of being attached. Sticks might be pushed underneath the dancer's cheeks or underneath the dense back muscles.

No matter how he was hooked up, a dancer would then be given an ornamental eagle-bone whistle to blow while he danced.

The dance would last for hours; each warrior's face lifted toward the sun while he blew his whistle.

It was a test of strength and courage in the face of horrible torture. If any warrior would cry out and ask to be cut down, he would be treated like a squaw for the rest of his life.

It's no wonder the soldiers and Indian scouts feared warriors with such courage and such powers to resist pain and suffering!

But Custer was still confident of victory. No superstitious ritual was going to frighten him. Let the Sioux see how much their medicine would help them against the charge of a force of cavalry!

For now, however, the soldiers rested, and Custer ordered the officers to have the men cook their rations over small fires. "Tell the men to make sure their fires make no large amount of smoke and to be sure to put them out before dark," he said.

The camp settled down for a while as the men ate their rations, and the officers gathered together by their tents to rest, swap stories, and even sing some songs.

That same night in the Indian village that was situated by the Little Bighorn River, well within the area that Custer and the generals had guessed it would be, Crazy Horse sat by his lodge and was satisfied.

He had a lot to be satisfied about because this was the greatest encampment the plains had ever seen. For months, Indians had been coming here to cast their lots with Crazy Horse and Sitting Bull.

Besides the Hunkpapa Sioux of Sitting Bull and the Oglalas of Crazy Horse, there were Cheyenne, Brulés, Sans Arcs, Santee, and a good number of other tribes. All the hostiles knew that the soldiers were out to get them, and even the agency Indians streamed back to be with their comrades. It was a mighty camp that stretched for three or four miles along the banks of the Little Bighorn River.

Like Custer, Crazy Horse felt confident of victory. Sitting Bull had told them that he had had a vision. He said that he had seen many soldiers with their heads down and their hats flying off, falling right into their camp. No one needed a holy man to tell them what this vision meant. It meant that the soldiers would come to their great village and be killed.

Not only that, on June 17th, Crazy Horse and his warriors had fought General Crook—who was supposed to be part of the trap that hoped to capture the Indians—and turned him around. He had retreated south after a fierce battle in the Rosebud River country in which the Indians, under Crazy Horse, had fought for the first time as a disciplined military force.

No more counting coups, no more show-off individual attacks. The Indians at last realized that fighting the white man was no longer a game, as it had been when they fought with each other. The white man fought to kill and so the Indian must do the same.

Crazy Horse knew that more soldiers were coming. The war was not yet over. That night, however, the Indians were in a celebrating mood. Let the soldiers come. Who could hope to win against such a great camp? There was dancing and feasting and singing, all through the night, with much riding between different individual camps and visiting old friends.

Sunday, June 25th, broke clear and warm. It was a typical summer day on the prairie. Everywhere the purple, yellow, and white prairie flowers bobbed in the breeze as if nodding good morning to the tired troopers of the Seventh Cavalry as they trotted by.

After the men had rested a bit the night before, Custer had ordered a night march. He had wanted to get as close as possible to the valley of the Little Bighorn this morning without actually entering it.

Custer wanted to do this because he knew that the village was somewhere in the valley, and he planned to attack it and round up the hostiles as soon as he found out its exact location. He was going to do this even though it would have been better to let the men rest for a day before going into battle. It also would have been wiser to wait for Terry and Gibbon to catch up. But he was sure the Indians knew they were there, and he was worried that they might escape if he waited any longer.

Furthermore, Custer knew as well as everybody else did that this was to be the last great fight with the hostiles. Whoever distinguished himself in this battle would come away with great glory. He was determined that it would be he and the Seventh Cavalry who would have that honor.

Also, he had been approached more than once by people who thought that he would make a good candidate for president. If he were the one who swept the plains clean of hostiles, it might sweep him into the White House!

Now, in the early-morning haze, Custer peered into the valley of the Little Bighorn from a high point, called Crow's Nest. He had joined his scouts there after they had told him that they could detect a big village about fifteen miles away by the Little Bighorn River.

But try as he might, Custer could not see the village even with a spy glass, and he told the scouts as much. "Yes, *Otoe* Sioux! *Otoe* Sioux!" cried the Ree Indian scouts. "*Otoe* Sioux. Plenty. Too many. Sioux everywhere."

A scout named Bloody Knife agreed. "We will find enough Sioux to keep us fighting for two or three days," he said.

But Custer just smiled. He knew Indian scouts to be cautious. "I guess we'll get through with them in one day," he said.

Just before noon, the sky became overcast and a light breeze sprang up, bringing with it the sweet smells of plum, crabapple, and wild roses. It almost, but not quite, hid the smell of sweaty horses, leather, and alkaline dust. The Seventh Cavalry now stood at the brink of the Little Bighorn valley at the entrance to a large draw that sloped down into it. Even though Custer did not see the village yet, he knew now that it was somewhere down by the Little Bighorn River.

The column started down the draw, tired, dusty men on tired, dusty horses. Although they couldn't see the waters of the Little Bighorn River itself from there, a line of trees indicated its bed. Custer waved a fringed arm and pointed to the southwest. He turned to one of his officers, Captain Benteen, and said, "Take three companies and scout that area. If you find any Indians, pitch in and send a rider to let us know."

But Benteen was doubtful. "Hadn't we better keep the regiment together, General?" he said. "If this is as big a camp as they say, we'll need every man we have."

Custer just looked at him and said, "You have your orders."

With an unhappy expression, Benteen prodded his horse and gave the command to move forward. The three companies of troopers trotted down the draw and headed southwest.

As soon as Benteen had left, Custer turned to Major Marcus Reno and ordered him to take another three companies down the south side of the draw.

He himself took five companies and left one to guard the ammunition wagons, which were slowly moving up to their rear. With his men, Custer rode on the north side of the draw.

So in three roughly parallel columns, the six hundred and eleven men of the Seventh Cavalry marched toward the Little Bighorn where Crazy Horse and three thousand warriors were waiting.

# 19
# Custer's Last Fight

**A**s the three columns moved toward the Little Bighorn, a scout reported to Custer that he had seen part of an Indian camp a little way north. Custer wheeled his column north and into a line of bluffs that hid from his view the river and any camp that might be there. His intention was to ride along the flank of where he believed the village to be. He knew that Reno would continue on his path and, with luck, end up at the other, or south, end of the village. He meant to ride until he could see the north end of the village and attack from there. This way the Indians would be caught between two forces and be trapped.

Benteen, in the meantime, would either attack from the southwest or cover any retreat of the Indians in that direction.

Custer and his men continued riding along the bluffs until they came to a spot where they could see the river. When they got there, the troopers looked in awe at the sight before their eyes.

There on the opposite side of the Little Bighorn stood circle after circle of tepees. More tepees than they had *ever* seen together in one spot! It was an immense village!

What Custer and his men didn't know, however, was that they were looking at just a small portion of it. They had no idea how big it *really* was!

But if Custer was worried, he didn't show it. Instead he looked back at his men and shouted, "We've caught them napping!"

In that first look at the village, Custer had seen only normal activity — no warriors milling about ready to charge them — only women, children, and old people going about their daily business.

The troopers found a small ravine that cut right down to the river. Custer looked back at his men. They were ready.

He gave the command to move forward and the 210 troopers under Custer's command went trotting down toward the valley of the Little Bighorn. . . .

Down in the village, hundreds of young children were splashing and swimming in the cool waters of the river while the older teenagers kept an eye on them. The women went about their work as they did every day, and the men were walking around the village visiting, talking, and wondering when the soldiers would come.

It was said the one called Long-hair was among them — the yellow-haired chief who had attacked the village on the Washita. But in spite of their wondering, it was a lazy afternoon and it seemed that there was peace and happiness all over the world. Many had gone to sleep late the night before because of all the dancing and singing and visiting that had lasted almost to the dawn.

It was now late afternoon and Crazy Horse had left his tepee and gone over to visit the Cheyenne camp which was at the north end of the great village.

Suddenly an Indian came whipping his horse fast into the camp. "Soldiers coming here!" he cried out. "Soldiers coming here!"

The cry rang out like a cannon shot through the sleepy village. Runners started to the other camps to spread the alarm. Warriors tumbled out of their tepees shouting to their women to bring their war ponies.

"Where? Where are the soldiers?" a woman with a baby on a cradleboard asked.

"Back there by the Hunkpapas!" shouted a warrior already mounted on his war pony.

Everyone was surprised. Dawn was the usual time to attack, not in the heat of the afternoon. But at the first hint of danger, the warriors rallied and the war cry *"Hoka-hey!"* rang through the air.

The Hunkpapas of Sitting Bull were camped at

the south end of the village, and it was here that the first troopers attacked.

It was Reno's three companies, which had been sent by Custer to seek out the village. They had reached the river and crossed over at a shallow spot and had spotted the village ahead of them. Now the long blue line was forming for the charge.

Sitting Bull mounted a black stallion and galloped among the lodges to "brave up" the warriors. Many of them were already riding to meet Reno's attack, but many others took the time to put on their warpaint and warrior's clothes. Crazy Horse was among these. He had heard the cry of alarm but he wanted to make sure his medicine was good. He dressed for war as he had always done. He was never one to panic in the face of danger.

Major Reno ordered the charge, and the troopers dashed forward. A cloud of dust appeared ahead of them, churned up by the Indian ponies riding hard to meet the soldiers. Suddenly bands of feathered fiends appeared out of the dust cloud as if by magic. They leased a volley of lead and arrows at Reno and his men, then wheeled their ponies to disappear into the swirl of battle. But as soon as one band disappeared, another took its place.

Reno hadn't expected this. He had expected that

the Indians would be routed as they had always been in the face of a strong cavalry charge. Instead, these Indians were making a stand and meeting his charge head-on.

And where was Custer? He had expected the colonel to be behind him. Custer had told him that the whole command would support him once he attacked the village. But Custer was nowhere to be seen and neither was Benteen, for that matter.

Again the Indians appeared through the dust, but now there were many more than before — yipping, screaming, firing their guns, unleashing their arrows, and not giving an inch.

In a near-panic, Reno stopped the charge and ordered his men to dismount. He had no wish to enter that deadly cloud of battle and be swallowed up within its center.

He and his men dashed for the cover of a nearby cottonwood grove. Here the Indians had the advantage over the dismounted troopers. Within minutes, the warriors poured into the woods and started to cut down Reno's men, one by one.

In a complete panic now, Reno and his men scampered back onto their horses and headed for the river. There was no time to find a place to cross. They simply galloped their horses right off the edge of a six-foot bank and plunged into the river, the Indians hot on their heels.

The warriors poured arrow after arrow into these helpless troopers as their horses swam in saddle-deep water. *"Yip-hoo!"* They made the game-killing cry as arrow after arrow found its target.

The lucky ones who weren't hit reached the other bank and scrambled up a steep incline to some high bluffs. Here at last they found some refuge, and with anything they could lay their hands on — cups, spoons, knives — they dug themselves in to repel an attack.

While this battle was still going on, a messenger came riding into the great camp. "More soldiers!" he cried. "Many more soldiers going down along the ridge on the other side of the river!" This was Custer and his men.

Crazy Horse heard the cry and dashed onto his war pony calling to the warriors. *"Hoka-hey!* It is a good day to fight! It is a good day to die! Strong hearts, brave hearts to the front! Weak hearts and cowards to the rear."

The warriors answered as one. *"Hoka-hey!"* they cried as they followed the light-haired one out of the camp, each warrior hitting the pony of the one ahead of him so that no one would turn back. . . .

At this point Custer was getting ready to charge down and take the camp by surprise.

But the surprise was on him, because no sooner had the troopers of the Seventh Cavalry spurred their horses forward, than two thousand warriors swarmed out of the village and across the river like angry bees from a hive.

Custer reared up his horse and stopped the advance. The other troopers did the same and wheeled about, waiting for a command. They had little time to spare, however, because the hordes of warriors were already raining arrows down upon them. A few of the troopers were hit immediately and slumped from their horses, feathered shafts sticking out of their bodies.

The troopers answered with a volley of bullets from their carbines and saw a number of Indians reel as if hit. But that was an old Indian trick, so no one could be sure he had hit his target.

Now the Seventh Cavalry, so disciplined just a moment before, began a desperate and scattered retreat back up the slopes from where they had just come. The Indians pressed them hard. The tired troopers wheeled, and fired over their shoulders as they made for higher ground. Their suntanned faces gray with dust, they sighted along their rifles — which felt hot and heavy in their hands — and shot at any target they could find. Arrows and now some bullets, too, buzzed past them, sounding like angry hornets. Deadly feathered shafts and hot lead found their marks as the men followed Custer up the ragged terrain.

As the soldiers scrambled up the sloping ground, they jumped off their horses and broke into scattered groups. Many were still shooting in a disciplined manner. But the troopers were no match for the hundreds and hundreds of warriors who were swarming wildly into their midst, on foot and on horseback, swinging warclubs, thrusting spears, firing guns, and zinging arrows. The dust churned up by the battle rose a hundred feet into the air and could be seen miles away.

Custer shouted to his men to form skirmish lines as the number of dead horses multiplied around them. He felt confident that Reno and Benteen would soon be coming. They could hold off the Indians until then.

He and his brother Tom, and Captain Yates, one of his officers, made for the top of the ridge as the rest of the men formed skirmish lines here and there. Custer, too, got off his horse and, together with Captain Yates, formed a defensive circle with fifty troopers using the bodies of dead horses as breast-works.

Tom's company was strung out below them and pouring lead into the Indians as fast as they could. But there were too many. Too many Sioux, Cheyenne, Arapaho, Blackfeet — too many Indians!

There was so much noise and confusion, so much dust, that it was hard to tell friend from foe. A few warriors were even cut down by arrows from their own people.

Now Custer and the men with him edged closer to the top of the ridge. If they could rally the men up here, they could escape to the rear.

While this was happening, Crazy Horse

whipped his war pony into a gallop at the head of a thousand warriors. They had not gone directly up the ridge to join the other warriors, but instead circled around and went up a ravine to the right of Custer, hidden from him and his men.

Crazy Horse was dressed, as always, for battle, like the man in his vision: stripped down to only his breechcloth, hailspots on his body, the lightning bolt down his cheek. One feather lay flat in his hair behind him, and the dried body of a red-backed hawk was set on his head.

With his heart singing the war song, his rifle ready in his hand, the light-haired one led his warriors up from the ravine and to the top of the ridge where Custer and the Seventh Cavalry were desperately fighting.

When they reached the top, they paused a moment and looked down at the backs of the blue-clad troopers. The troopers, seeing them instantly, looked up with startled eyes.

Crazy Horse saw some white chiefs among the soldiers there — they were the ones dressed in fringed buckskin — but did not recognize the one they called Long-hair. No matter, if Long-hair was here he would be killed along with everybody else.

With a great cry, Crazy Horse and the warriors charged down onto the dusty, tired, and frightened troopers. They were hot for the fight and the soldiers' bullets were little more than annoying things to be brushed aside like insects on a summer day.

159

Custer glanced up the ridge at the cry from his men. He saw a horde of mounted warriors riding down upon them. Bedecked with feathers, wearing buffalo headdresses and war bonnets, their painted ponies sleek and strong, the warriors crashed into the men like a mighty ocean wave.

If Custer noticed the warrior with the light hair and the red lightning bolt down his cheek, he would have given him little thought. He was fighting for his life against overwhelming odds. One Indian, more or less, would make little difference.

But he knew he would pull through. He always did. It was Custer's luck. How could the boy general who had made charge after charge in battle, and had escaped harm even when his horses were shot dead under him, die here on this barren ridge?

No, it was unthinkable.

As the great wave of warriors engulfed him and his men, he took out his two revolvers from their holsters. His sporting rifle was empty and lay useless on the ground beside him.

Taking careful aim and shouting encouragement to his men, he calmly shot off round after round into the screaming, painted, savage horde that now surrounded the little band near the crest of the ridge.

"*Yip-hoo!*" Crazy Horse made the game-killing cry as he spurred his pony and rode down any soldier in his way. His Winchester barked once, twice, three times as he wheeled and twisted his pony around in a tight circle.

*Hou!* It was like killing buffalo!

But some brave soldiers were still firing their rifles in the kneeling position, taking careful aim. A great cloud of dust was raised by the Indians' ponies as they circled the dwindling number of troopers on the top of the ridge. The others along the ridge had all been killed or were about to be. Even though Crazy Horse guessed they were winning, it was hard to see how the battle was going. The dust and the smoke from the rifles blocked out the near horizon.

Suddenly Crazy Horse saw that there was just the small circle of men on the ridge top. There was a white chief standing there like a sheaf of corn with all the ears fallen around him. He wore a buckskin shirt and a red tie. He was firing two revolvers at the circling warriors, and smiling. *Hou!* This chief was not like the others!

Arrows slashed by him but none had hit. Was this chief also a possessor of strong medicine as he was? Did he, by some magic, force the arrows away from his body? Crazy Horse spurred his horse through the dust and his screaming comrades to get closer.

Then he saw the soldier chief fire at a warrior riding by. Another warrior aimed his gun at the white chief just as the white chief clicked his empty revolvers. He had fired his last shots but

Custer's Last Stand

instead of despairing, he threw back his head and laughed — a shrill, high laugh as if laughing at a good joke.

The laugh was cut short as two bullets hit the brave officer, and he crumpled down among his men. Soon the only movement on that hill of death was the white chief's flag fluttering in the wind.

Suddenly there were no more soldiers left. A powerful silence came over the ridge that seemed to fill the ears just as the noise of battle had. Then just as suddenly, the silence was broken as the warriors yowled and yipped and rode around the hilltop firing arrow after arrow, bullet after bullet into the dead bodies. It was as if they were sorry that the soldiers had only died once.

Crazy Horse had no wish to join in this orgy of hate and he spurred his pony and went back down to the river. When he got there, he was told that none of the soldiers had even come near the village; the warriors had met them on the ridges above.

Crazy Horse should have been happy at the day's work, but instead, a strange sadness overcame him. He went back to the ridge of the dead.

The women and some braves were taking the last of the clothes off the dead men. The rest lay naked and white like buffalo fat on the grassy ground. They looked so pitiful now, so helpless, that Crazy Horse felt bad for them. Why did they have to come shooting at the people who only wanted to be left alone?

He dismounted and walked slowly among the bodies, looking for the white chief who had been so brave. Crazy Horse found him at the spot where he had last seen him go down.

He, too, was naked, but unlike the others, the white chief was not scalped. His hair was blond like corn but cut short. Crazy Horse seemed to recognize him as the one he had seen sleeping underneath the cottonwood tree. It might well be Long-hair — but then why was not so great a chief scalped?

Then he saw that the officer's hair was thin at the back where the hair grew in a circle. Crazy Horse understood. He was not scalped because of this.

To the Sioux, the circle was the magical part of the scalp and the one that was most prized. The sun was round, the moon was round, even their shields which protected them against their enemies' arrows and bullets were round. The circle was *wakan* — sacred, and in taking and owning a scalp, a warrior took and owned his enemy's power. But no one wanted the scalp of this soldier chief because it was thin at the crown where all the power lay. *Hou!* It was true.

Crazy Horse remounted his horse and trotted slowly back to the village. His heart was glad that the warriors had shown so much courage and discipline that day. But it was also sad. Somehow he knew that even though they had won this battle, they were destined to lose the war.

They may kill his body, he mused, but they would never kill his spirit! *"Hoka-hey!"* Crazy Horse kicked his pony into a fast run and went galloping down into the village so that all could see the pride of a Sioux warrior!

# *Epilogue*

**M**ajor Reno and his remaining troops were rescued by Captain Benteen, who had returned from his scouting mission just in time to join in the battle on the bluffs which had lasted throughout the night and into the next day.

In any case, the Indians suddenly broke off the fight and the whole huge camp pulled up their belongings and marched south toward the Bighorn mountains. There had been enough killing, and their hearts could take no more.

On the night of the 26th, the day after the Custer battle, Terry and Gibbon finally showed up, and the next day learned the terrible news that Custer and all the men with him had been killed.

But in the end, Crazy Horse was right. Even though the Indians had won the battle, they were destined to lose the war. After the Little Bighorn battle, the Indians once more broke up into scattered tribes. Sitting Bull finally drifted up to Canada with the bulk of the hostiles, and Crazy Horse, with only six hundred warriors, headed for the Black Hills to continue the now-hopeless fight against the whites.

A little more than a year later, Crazy Horse was killed at a place called Fort Robinson. He had turned himself in peaceably, but he had no sooner gotten to the fort, than the soldiers tried to force him into a jail cell.

Crazy Horse couldn't stand the thought of being cooped up like that. He broke loose and started to fight. But he was hopelessly trapped, and the fight soon ended when one of the guards stabbed him with a bayonette.

At last, in death, the two warriors had finally come to the ends of their paths. . . .

# Bibliography

Ambrose, Stephen E. *Crazy Horse and Custer.* New York, 1975.

Bleeker, Sonia. *The Sioux Indians: Hunters and Warriors of the Plains.* New York, 1962.

Connell, Evan S. *Son of the Morning Star.* New York, 1984.

Custer, Elizabeth Bacon. *Boots and Saddles: or, Life in Dakota with General Custer.* University of Oklahoma, 1961.

Custer, Elizabeth Bacon. *Tenting on the Plains.* University of Oklahoma, 1971.

Erdoes, Richard. *The Sun Dance People: The Plains Indians, Their Past and Present.* New York, 1972.

Garst, Shannon. *Crazy Horse.* Boston, Massachusetts, 1950.

Graham, Col. W.A. *The Custer Myth: A Source Book of Custeriana.* New York, 1953.

Greene, Jerome A. *Evidence and the Custer Enigma: A Reconstruction of Indian-Military History.* Reno, Nevada, 1973.

Hinman, Eleanor. "Oglala Sources on the Life of Crazy Horse," *Nebraska History. Vol 57, No. 1,* Lincoln Nebraska 1976.

Hoig, Stan. *The Battle of the Washita: The Sheridan-Custer Indian Campaign of 1867 – 69.* Lincoln, Nebraska, 1979.

Jones, Douglas C. *The Court-Martial of George Armstrong Custer.* New York, 1976.

Mattes, Merrill J. *Indians, Infants and Infantry: Andrew and Elizabeth Burt on the Frontier.* Denver, Colorado, 1960.

Merington, Marguerite, ed. *The Custer Story: The Life and Intimate Letters of General George A. Custer and His Wife Elizabeth.* New York, 1950.

Monaghan, Jay. *Custer: The Life of General George Armstrong Custer.* Lincoln, Nebraska, 1959.

Reusswig, William. *A Picture Report of the Custer Fight.* New York, 1967.

Sandoz, Mari. *Crazy Horse: The Strange Man of the Oglalas.* Lincoln, Nebraska, 1942.

Scudder, Ralph E. *Custer Country.* Portland, Oregon, 1963.

Walker, Judson Elliott. *Campaigns of General Custer.* New York, 1966.